The Princeton Review®

GMAT & GRE Math Made Easy:

Understanding Quantitative Reasoning for Math-Phobic Grad School Applicants

By John Fulmer

princetonreview.com

Penguin Random House

The Princeton Review
110 East 42nd Street, 7th Floor
New York, NY 10017

Copyright © 2022 by TPR Education IP
Holdings, LLC. All rights reserved.

Published in the United States by Penguin
Random House LLC, New York.

ISBN: 978-0-593-51656-0
ISSN: 2833-4493

GMAT® is a registered trademark of the
Graduate Management Admission Council.

GRE® is a registered trademark of the
Educational Testing Service (ETS). This
product is not endorsed or approved by ETS.

The Princeton Review is not affiliated with
Princeton University.

Editor: Chris Chimera
Production Editors: Nina Mozes and Sarah Litt
Production Artists: Deborah Weber

Printed in the United States of America.

10 9 8 7 6 5 4 3 2 1

The Princeton Review Publishing Team

Rob Franek, Editor-in-Chief
David Soto, Senior Director, Data Operations
Stephen Koch, Senior Manager, Data Operations
Deborah Weber, Director of Production
Jason Ullmeyer, Production Design Manager
Jennifer Chapman, Senior Production Artist
Selena Coppock, Director of Editorial
Orion McBean, Senior Editor
Aaron Riccio, Senior Editor
Meave Shelton, Senior Editor
Chris Chimera, Editor
Patricia Murphy, Editor
Laura Rose, Editor
Alexa Schmitt Bugler, Editorial Assistant

Penguin Random House Publishing Team

Tom Russell, VP, Publisher
Alison Stoltzfus, Publishing Director
Brett Wright, Senior Editor
Emily Hoffman, Associate Managing Editor
Ellen Reed, Production Manager
Suzanne Lee, Designer
Eugenia Lo, Publishing Assistant

For customer service,
please contact
editorialsupport@review.com,
and be sure to include:

- full title of the book

- ISBN

- page number

Acknowledgments

The acknowledgments are, without a doubt, the most challenging part of any book to write. All books, no matter their length, are a team effort. And there are so many members of that team—from the editors to the casual acquaintances who smile politely while you ramble on about your project. So, you grapple with the simultaneous fears of failing to acknowledge someone integral and over-acknowledging to such an extent that you wind up writing another book.

After some reflection and paring, there are two groups of people that I would especially like to thank—those who were instrumental in the production of this book itself and those who helped shape my own mathematical journey.

The powerhouse editorial team at the Princeton Review, especially Selena Coppock and Chris Chimera, believed in the mission of this book. Both gave me the time and leeway to explore how I could best convey my ideas. Deborah Weber's awesome book design and layout made the book more readable. Nina Mozes and Sarah Litt paid careful attention to each page. I appreciate everyone's hard work.

From the Princeton Review Product team, I like to thank Shadna Wise and Blaise Mortiz, who helped me to meet book deadlines and fit this project into my schedule of other projects.

No math journey takes place in isolation. We all need teachers and mentors, as well as friends and family, to provide encouragement. So, I'd also like to acknowledge a few people who were instrumental in my math journey.

First, I'd like to thank my parents, who paid for my math education. They were also there in those early years to quiz me when I needed to know my times tables and geometry formulas!

I'd also like to thank the faculty of the mathematics department at Case Western Reserve University circa the mid-1980s for providing such fine instruction. In particular, I'd like to thank the late Professors Wojbor Woyczynski and Charles Welles. Even though both knew that I was never going to be a research mathematician, each provided ample guidance and encouragement.

Finally, I'd like to thank the many students I have taught and tutored over the years. I hope that they've learned as much from me as I have from them.

Contents

Get More
(Free) Content
at **PrincetonReview.com/prep**

As easy as **1·2·3**

1 Go to PrincetonReview.com/prep or scan the **QR code** and enter the following ISBN for your book:
9780593516560

2 Answer a few simple questions to set up an exclusive Princeton Review account. *(If you already have one, you can just log in.)*

3 Enjoy access to your **FREE** content!

Once you've registered, you can...

- Get our take on any recent or pending updates to the GMAT and GRE.
- Take a free practice test for the GMAT and GRE.

- Download bonus chapters on crucial content for the GMAT and GRE.
- Check to see if there have been any corrections or updates to this edition.

Need to report a potential **content** issue?

Contact **EditorialSupport@review.com** and include:

- full title of the book
- ISBN
- page number

Need to report a **technical** issue?

Contact **TPRStudentTech@review.com** and provide:

- your full name
- email address used to register the book
- full book title and ISBN
- Operating system (Mac/PC) and browser (Chrome, Firefox, Safari, etc.)

The **Princeton**Review®

CONSIDERING A GMAT® OR GRE® PREP COURSE?

Choose Your Program

Find the perfect solution for your test prep needs.

GMAT PREP*

- GMAT 700+
- GMAT Fundamentals
- GMAT Self-Paced
- GMAT Tutoring

GRE PREP*

- GRE 162+
- GRE Fundamentals
- GRE Self-Paced
- GRE Tutoring

Ace Your Exams

Maximize your scores using a wide range of services. (options vary per package)

- Score improvement guarantee*
- Live instruction by test experts (not for Self-Paced courses)
- Personalized test prep
- Practice tests and drills
- Online lessons
- Interactive video lessons and adaptive drills
- and more!

Contact us to learn more at
www.PrincetonReview.com
1-800-2-REVIEW

Foreword

So, here's my confession.

One of my earliest memories of math is not a good one. My third-grade teacher quizzed us daily on our multiplication tables using records. (Yes, records were still a thing when I was in primary school.) She had a series of records in which a stentorian voice announced a multiplication problem. There was a pause to write down the answer, followed by another problem: 7 times 8, pause, 5 times 6.

The first few records in the series were fine because there were long pauses between problems. You had time to remember the answer, write it down, look out the window, and remember that you were taking a quiz before the next problem was announced. As the series of records progressed, however, the pauses became shorter. Eventually, there was a near constant barrage of multiplication problems being hurled at the class. If you missed a problem, you were done. I fell behind on more than one quiz.

When we complained to our teacher—whom I genuinely liked, by the way—that the record was too fast, she wasn't very sympathetic. "You need to know your times tables fast," she told us without a hint of a smile. A few students cried.

That day in the third grade didn't turn me against math. In fact, I love math! I get a visceral thrill when I solve a hard problem. However, I did learn that it's okay to take your time and that math can be challenging.

For college, I went to Case Western Reserve University in Cleveland with the intention of majoring in biochemistry. However, I got placed into an honors level course on vector calculus, which is usually the third calculus course that math, science, and engineering majors take. On the first day of class, the professor walked in and announced, "I just want to check that everyone has the right background for this course. So, here's a quiz that you need to complete tonight to stay in the class." As great as my high school calculus class had been, there were a few things that I didn't know. So, I went back to the dorm, taught myself a few things, passed the quiz, and stayed in the class.

The professor for that course, Wojbor Woyczynski, was a well-regarded probability theorist. My fellow students and I weren't exactly sure why he was teaching this class when he could have been teaching more advanced courses. But I really liked that class. I liked it so much that I decided to major in math.

I wound up taking four more courses with Professor Woyczynski. At the conclusion of the fourth course, he informed us that he'd been teaching the sequence of courses that math majors take so he could prepare us to take an advanced probability course for undergraduates. That was one challenging probability course!

After I graduated, I went to grad school for Political Science, which I was also majoring in. I went to the University of Rochester, where I used game theory to study international relations. More importantly, I had the opportunity to teach two summer courses while I was there and learned that I really loved teaching.

That love of teaching eventually led me to The Princeton Review. That was almost 30 years ago. By this point, I've taught hundreds of classes, tutored hundreds of students one on one, and trained many of our teachers both here in the U.S. and at some of our international locations in India, Thailand, Taiwan, and the UAE. I've met a lot of very interesting people along the way. (And I was once slapped by a monkey in India.)

I've learned a lot from my students about how people understand math and, more importantly, how people *learn* math. I've learned that math instruction requires patience on both the part of the teacher and the student. I've always tried to keep in mind that math can be very challenging, and I've also learned a lot about how people respond to a challenging math problem.

I've also learned a lot about how the test-writers of the GMAT and the GRE write math questions. I've tried to use that knowledge for good, which, in this case, means helping test-takers get better scores. This book contains a lot of what I've learned from these and other experiences.

So that's my math journey. I hope you'll find this book helpful and make it part of your math journey.

John Fulmer
Content Director, GMAT & GRE
The Princeton Review

PART I

Preliminaries

CHAPTER 1

Introduction

Greetings

If you are like most people reading this book, you've discovered that you need to take either the GMAT or GRE soon. You've probably also learned a few things about the test you need to take, including that both tests have math sections.

The discovery that both tests have math sections may have led to a very specific reaction, which we'll characterize as "Ugh! Math!" We'll allow for the possibility that your language may have been more colorful! That's okay!

Math often doesn't elicit fond memories or happy thoughts. For many people, math causes feelings more akin to anxiety, fear, dread, or outright panic. I once had a student describe his feelings when he reads a math problem like this: "It's as though my brain has been put in a dishwasher. I forget everything. My mind just goes blank." If that's you, this book is a judgement-free zone!

Let's just see if we can get through this little math adventure together so you can take your test and be done with it. If you forget everything that you've learned in this book as soon as you get the score that you need, well, judgement-free zone.

Let's start with a somewhat open secret. The math sections of the GMAT and the GRE don't actually test math.

Wait! What?

The test-writers (ETS for the GRE and ACT for the GMAT) don't refer to the math sections of their tests as math sections. They refer to them as Quantitative sections. Does that matter? Maybe the test-writers just like to use bigger words?[1]

---

[1] The GRE test-writers most decidedly like to use bigger words. Half the verbal section of the GRE is geared toward evaluating the extent to which your lexicon is sesquipedalian. But, as this is a book about math, we'll leave the verbal discourse for another day.

The choice of word used to title the section does matter. Tests exist to assess knowledge or abilities or both. Most of the tests that you've taken in school were designed to assess your knowledge. A fact-based history test, for example, might aim to assess whether you've learned certain facts about U.S. Presidents, such as who was the first president (George Washington)[2]; which president served in Congress after his presidency (John Quincy Adams); who was the first Vice President to assume office after the death of his predecessor (His Accidency John Tyler). A more involved test might test both knowledge and abilities. For example, a history test that includes essays assesses not only which facts you know but also how well you synthesize those facts to argue a point. It also indirectly tests how well you write.

In the same vein, a math section would primarily aim to assess your knowledge of math facts and formulas. But the GMAT and GRE test-writers are interested in more than whether you know the formula for the area of a circle. (It's $A = \pi r^2$, by the way.) They are interested in assessing your quantitative reasoning ability.

What's that and how does it differ from math? I'm glad you asked!

What is Quantitative Reasoning?

Let's look at some problems.

I know, I know. This is an introduction, and introductions are supposed to be light reading. But it's really important that you understand the difference between a test that assesses math knowledge and one that assesses quantitative reasoning. We'll avoid doing anything too crazy for now.

Let's look at a problem that assesses something simple such as whether you know a formula. No question on either the GMAT or GRE would simply ask for the formula. If the test-writers wanted to know whether you knew a formula, they would construct a problem that would make you use that formula.

---

[2] Assuming that we are starting the count after the ratification of the current Constitution.

Reasoning with Formulas

Here's an example:

> If the radius of the circle with center O is 4, what is the area of the circle?
>
> (A) 2π
> (B) 4π
> (C) 8π
> (D) 16π
> (E) 32π

Let's forget about how to solve this problem for a minute. This problem would be unlikely to appear on either the GMAT or the GRE. The issue, from the perspective of the test-writers, is that this problem mostly assesses math knowledge (Do you know the formula for the area of a circle? Do you know how to use that formula?) rather than quantitative reasoning.

Now, let's look at the solution to clarify why this problem mostly tests math knowledge.

The problem asks for the area of a circle and supplies the radius of that circle. The area of any circle can be found using the formula $A = \pi r^2$. To find the area of this circle, just substitute 4 for the value of r in the formula: $A = \pi(4^2) = 16\pi$.

If we made the problem a little harder, the test-writers of the GMAT or GRE might start to show some interest. Consider this version of the problem.

> If the circumference of the circle with center O is 8π, what is the area of the circle?
>
> (A) 2π
> (B) 4π
> (C) 8π
> (D) 16π
> (E) 32π

Now the problem includes an extra step, and you need to know two formulas to solve it. More importantly, from the perspective of the test-writers, you need to be able to connect what you were told about the circumference of the circle to the goal of finding the area of the circle. Making connections is part of quantitative reasoning and that makes the test-writers of the GMAT or GRE more likely to include this problem.

Let's think about that for a moment before we solve the problem. Let's take an (somewhat) ahistorical[3] journey back in time. We're going to be taking a number of these journeys in this book, so get used to them!

Geometry is one of the oldest branches of mathematics. Nature doesn't exactly contain perfect shapes, but with a bit of abstraction (a key part of mathematical reasoning, by the way), one can certainly start to see the basic shapes such as circles and quadrilaterals that we all take for granted. Circles are particularly plentiful. Just look at the moon. Or walk around a tree. Being surrounded by less-than-perfect geometric shapes no doubt led some ancient geometer somewhere to start thinking about making those shapes more perfect.

So, our ancient geometer starts to draw circles on the ground and starts to notice that some circles are bigger than others. Our ancient geometer starts to puzzle out the relationship between the area of those circles and the diameter of those circles. Eventually, our ancient geometer is joined by other ancient geometers, and they start to work out ways to measure the area of the circle and the distance around the circle. They start to describe circles in terms of their characteristics, such as their center, diameter, and radius. One day, someone notices that the ratio of the circumference of the circle and its diameter is always the same, no matter the size of the circle. We're not yet in the age of what we would think of as formulas, but by the time of the Babylonians and the Egyptians, this ratio, which we know as π, can be calculated to several digits. That's a very useful thing to know when you have a need to construct buildings!

---

[3] The journey is ahistorical because someone who has studied the history of mathematics will no doubt be tempted, at times, to wag their finger and declaim in horror, "It didn't really happen that way!" Tut-tut. Who cares? There are times when the story serves a purpose, even if the details are somewhat fictive. These ahistorical journeys will help us to see certain connections in math that will aid in our understanding of quantitative reasoning. That, in turn, will help you to prepare for the GMAT or GRE.

The point of this little story is not that the test-writers expect you know where π comes from. However, they do expect you to make connections between different pieces of information provided in problems. They expect you to be able to relate the results of one calculation to another. They expect you to be able to solve problems that include multiple steps because making connections is part of quantitative reasoning!

Now, let's solve that problem.

The problem states that the circumference of the circle is 8π and asks for the area of the circle. A good starting point is to write down any formulas that might be needed. Formulas give us ways to assess what we know, and that can help us to determine what else we might need to find to make the formula work. For this problem, we need two formulas: the circumference of a circle, $C = 2\pi r$, and the area of a circle, $A = \pi r^2$. Note that both formulas involve the radius of the circle. That's our connection. We can use what we know, the circumference of the circle, to find the radius of the circle: $8\pi = 2\pi r$ and $r = 4$. Now, substitute the value for the radius into the area formula: $A = \pi(4^2) = 16\pi$. The answer to our question is (D).

Is This Even Math?

Ready to see a problem that assesses quantitative reasoning ability? Don't worry, we won't make this first one too hard.

> Each of the integers from 0 to 8, inclusive, is written on a separate slip of blank paper and the nine slips of paper are dropped into a bowl. If the slips of paper are drawn one at a time, without replacement, what is the minimum number of slips that must be drawn to guarantee that two of the slips of paper have a sum of 9 ?
>
> (A) 4
> (B) 5
> (C) 6
> (D) 7
> (E) 8

First off—what?

It's not a traditional math problem. Or, is it?

The problem certainly has a discernible mathematical component to it. After all, we do need to count! However, it's not an algebra question. It's not a geometry question. It's not a question about a standard arithmetic topic such as a ratio or an average.

It's more like a logic problem, isn't it?

Before we dive into the solution and discuss why the test-writers would be interested in putting such a question on the test, here's a bit of good news. This type of problem isn't very common on either the GMAT or GRE. For either test, you'd likely see at most one such question.

Now, let's solve it!

Let's start by clarifying some terminology used in the question. We'll have more to say about some of these terms in other parts of this book, but we'll cover a few basics for now. After all, you can't expect to solve a problem if you don't fully understand the problem!

The problem refers to the numbers that are written on the slips of paper as integers. **Integers** are just **whole numbers**. Integers can be positive, negative, or zero. So, the numbers we are using in this problem are 0, 1, 2, 3, 4, 5, 6, 7, and 8. The problem helpfully tells us that we are dealing with 9 numbers. Glad we didn't have to count those numbers!

The problem uses the terms *one at a time* and *without replacement* to describe the way in which the slips of paper are drawn from the bowl. These phrases are mostly technical requirements. Lots of math questions include words, phrases, and conditions that are technical requirements. If you remove these words or phrases, you could change the answer. Test-writers are very careful about how they word their questions. They don't want any of the test-takers coming back and saying "Hey! I couldn't solve this problem because it didn't specify...." Here, for example, if you were allowed to put one or more slips of paper back into the bowl after you drew it out, well, that's going to be a much harder problem!

Next, the problem asks for the *minimum number*. Again, that's sort of a technical requirement of the problem. Suppose that 9 was one of the answer choices. You certainly could draw out all 9 of the slips of paper and know that you got a pair, such as 1 and 8, that have a sum of 9. So, the problem isn't asking us to find any old answer that will work. We want the smallest number that's included in the answer choices that works.

To back up the idea that we need to find the minimum number, the problem also uses the word *must*. That's a strong word. We're going to have more to say about the words *must* and *could* and how they are used in math problems. For now, we can just say that the use of the word *must* is reinforcing that we need to find the minimum number.

Now that the vocab review is out of the way, let's start writing down pairs of numbers that have a sum of 9. Note that we can't pair 0 with any of the other numbers to get a sum of 9, so we'll need to worry about 0 separately. But the other numbers can be paired as follows:

$$1 + 8 = 9$$

$$2 + 7 = 9$$

$$3 + 6 = 9$$

$$4 + 5 = 9$$

Imagine that we constructed 4 boxes into which we are going to place each slip of paper after we take it out of the bowl. Each box can contain only the numbers from one of the pairs we just listed. We'll label each box with the pair of numbers it can contain. Here's what that looks like:

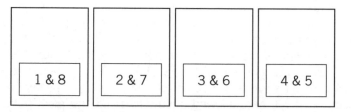

Now we need to add one more box because we need a place to put zero if we pick it.

0	1 & 8	2 & 7	3 & 6	4 & 5

Let's start drawing numbers and putting them into the boxes. We could get really lucky and pick two numbers that have a sum of 9, such as 1 and 8. However, we aren't interested in the fewest possible numbers we could pick that *could* give us a sum of 9. We're actually interested in the fewest possible numbers we could pick that *must* give us a sum of 9.

So, let's see how many numbers we could pick before we must place two numbers into one box, thus guaranteeing that we have drawn two numbers with a sum of 9. Let's suppose that by some fluke we just happen to draw the numbers in order. So, the first number we draw is 0. Then, we draw 1, followed by 2, followed by 3, followed by (you guessed it) 4. We have now drawn 5 slips of paper from the bowl. Each of our boxes now has 1 slip of paper in it and none of our boxes are empty.

What happens when we draw a sixth number from the bowl? No matter what number we draw, the slip of paper it is written on is going to go in a box that already has a slip of paper in it. We set up our boxes (other than our weird 0 box) so that the numbers that go into each box sum to 9. So, when we select the sixth number, we are guaranteed that one pair of numbers has a sum of 9. Since we selected as many numbers as we could before getting a pair that has a sum of 9, we have also proven that the minimum number of slips of paper that we can draw to guarantee that we have drawn a pair of numbers with our desired sum is 6. The answer to our question is (C).

You may have already worked out the answer before you read the solution. If so, that's good on two counts. First, it's always good to try to solve a problem on your own before reading a solution. We'll have more to say about that in the next chapter.

Second, if you worked out the answer before reading the solution, it means that you likely engaged in some quantitative reasoning!

Some questions that you encounter on the GMAT or GRE are based on topics or principles that are typically encountered in higher level mathematics courses. The test-writers don't expect you to know the sophisticated principles on which the problem is based. (Of course, if you do know the principle, it may give you an additional way to solve the problem!) The principles used in these problems are ones that someone who has what we'll describe as "math acumen" could figure out. The existence of such problems on the test is part of the interest on the part of the test-writers in measuring quantitative reasoning. Keep in mind, however, that most questions on the GMAT or GRE involve principles and topics that are more well-known!

The solution to our last problem made use of something called the Pigeonhole Principle, which is often used in proofs of math theorems. There's a simple version of the principle and a more complicated version. The simple version, which is what our solution used, can be passed off as common sense. Here's how the simple version of the Pigeonhole Principle works.

Suppose that you had six pigeons but only five pigeonholes to keep them in. What must be true of at least one of the pigeonholes? Right, at least one of the pigeonholes must contain at least two pigeons. If you started placing the pigeons into the pigeonholes, you'd be fine placing each pigeon into its own pigeonhole at first. You could do that for five of the pigeons. But now, you need to do something with that sixth pigeon. You'd need to put it into a pigeonhole with another pigeon. Let's hope that they get along!

Of course, you could also divide up the pigeons in ways that don't make use of all the available pigeonholes. You could, for example, place three pigeons each in two of the pigeonholes. Notice that when we asked our question about what must be true of the pigeonholes, we asked what must be true of *at least one* of the pigeonholes. The language of mathematics requires precision. You're going to see a lot of that in the GMAT and GRE problems that we look at. If you've ever wondered why a math problem was worded in a certain way, it's probably because it had to be worded that way to avoid logical fallacies or multiple solutions.

In case you're curious, here's how the simple form of the Pigeonhole Principle might be stated in a math text:

If $n + 1$ objects, where n is an integer, are placed into n boxes, at least one box has at least two objects in it.

Common sense, right?

It certainly doesn't seem like something important enough to count as a component of quantitative reasoning. Yet, we used it as the basis for a problem that either the GMAT or GRE would consider difficult. Mathematicians use the Pigeonhole Principle to prove all sorts of advanced ideas. It can also be used to prove fun observations, such as for every 27-word sequence in the U.S. Constitution, at least two words start with the same letter!

And, if you need more proof that simple ideas can lead to a lot of mathematics, consider that Euclid based plane geometry on only five postulates. Moreover, because he was suspicious of one of those postulates, he mostly used only the first four in his proofs!

CHAPTER 2

How to Study Math

Before we get into the nitty-gritty of some of the content that you need to know for the test, how to apply that content to problems, and how to demonstrate to the test-writers that you do indeed possess quantitative reasoning ability (aka the ability to pick the correct answers!), we need to discuss how to study math. If you are like most readers of this book, you've probably struggled with math in the past. You may have felt like you hit a brick wall when you look at problems. Or, you might see so many ways to get a problem started that you freeze in fear of picking the wrong approach. You may worry whether the way that you want to do the problem is the fastest way.

Or, to put all those thoughts into the context of a geometry problem, you might think, "But, I know all the formulas and rules! Why can't I figure this problem out?"

There's no denying that math involves a lot of rules! There are also a lot of definitions and formulas. There are also a great many algorithms designed to solve very specific problems. For example, you may remember a step-by-step procedure for factoring a quadratic equation or doing long division.

Because there are so many rules, and definitions, and formulas, you may be tempted to get to work making flashcards and start memorizing. Well, good! You will almost certainly need to do that.

However, one mistake that I see students make all the time is that they spend so much time memorizing rules, or reviewing notes, or reading about the content of the test that they never spend any time solving problems! Getting ready for a quantitative reasoning test can't be accomplished by simply reading and memorizing. You also need to spend substantial time doing math!

Suppose you wanted to learn to play golf. You certainly need to learn the rules and strategies. So, you might buy a couple of books about the rules so you can learn all about what you should do if your ball lands in the rough, a sand trap, or the water.[1] Those same books will also

---

[1] Yes, this was mostly my experience when I tried to learn to play golf. Rumor has it that some people are quite adept at getting the ball into the hole. I wasn't one of them, and I'm okay with that!

tell you how to hold the club when you swing and describe your stance when you putt. But you're not going to stop at reading some books, are you? Unless you happen to be a golf prodigy, your first visit to the golf course is likely to be a miserable experience if your preparations were confined to reading about how to tee off and putt. If you're like most new golfers, you'll take lessons. You'll hire the pro to tell you what is wrong with your swing. You'll also spend a lot of time at the driving range, and some (or all, in my case) of that time will be frustrating.

Studying math is a lot like learning to play golf because studying math is also a hands-on experience. You need to use those formulas, apply those rules, and push the boundaries of those definitions!

Let's look at some specific actions that you can (and should) incorporate into your preparations for the Quantitative sections of the GMAT or GRE. Think of these actions as the principles of highly effective math study.

Do More Than Read

Hey, I'm thrilled that you're reading this book! I really am!

However, I know that no matter how well-crafted my prose and no matter how cogent my math explanations, it won't be enough on its own to get you a good score on your GMAT or GRE. This book isn't a math travelogue. We need to take this journey together. I can serve as a guide who can point out common pitfalls so you can avoid common missteps. However, you also need to take the journey with me.

To hearken back to our golf analogy, you can't just read this book and expect to be prepared for your test. You'll also need to do practice problems and take practice tests. You'll need to learn from your mistakes.

Do More Than Memorize

Let's say that you wanted to add a word to your vocabulary. What would you do?

Let's think about an actual example. I choose the word *anent* for us to learn.

Seriously, anent is an actual word. It's really old. It was used in *Beowulf*. It almost died out for a while, then it came back, and now, sadly, it is once again in decline. Its frequency of use has declined markedly since 1920. Google says so...so it must be true. I've been on a quest to bring anent back for more than 30 years, so I had to use it in this book!

If you haven't already looked up the word, that would probably be your first step.

If you were to look up anent, you'd discover that it's a preposition and that it means *concerning* or *with regard to*. (Now you can see the utility of the word, can't you? Why would one ever want to say w*ith regard to* when a simple five-letter word will do the trick?)

Next, you'd probably want to read some sample sentences such as:

> Anent the city council's recent plan to pave a portion of Stewart Lake Park, I must object because this land is an important habitat for local wildlife.

> Or

> Some find the distinguished professor's research anent world affairs guided more by utopian idealism than the honest evaluation of events.

Now comes the important part, though. To really own the word, you need to use it in your own sentences.

Learning math definitions and formulas works much the same way. However, there's one extra step. To learn a math definition or formula, you'll also often need to ask questions about its use.

Let's say that you want to learn what a **prime number** is.

You might create a flashcard that uses a standard definition such as "A prime number is an integer that is only divisible by 1 and itself."

Sounds great! We're good to go, right?

Well, not quite. You might want to add some prime numbers to your flashcard in the same way that you might add sample sentences to a vocabulary flashcard. If you are being methodical, which is part of quantitative reasoning by the way, you might list the prime numbers in order. So, you write 2, 3, 5, 7, 11... on your flashcard.

But we're still not quite there in terms of learning what a prime number is. Now it's time to ask yourself some questions. For example:

Can fractions such as $\frac{1}{2}$ or decimals such as 0.75 be prime? No. The definition of prime states that a prime is an integer, and integers don't have any fractional or decimal parts.

Is every prime odd? No. Our list of primes included 2.

Is 2 the only even prime number? Yes. The definition of prime states that a prime is an integer that is only divisible by itself and 1. Every even number greater than 2 is divisible by 2, so those even numbers are not prime.

Is 1 prime? No. In school you might have been told that 1 is not prime because 1 is only divisible by 1. The actual reason is a little more complicated. Mathematicians decided to define 1 as not prime because several important results in number theory would break if 1 were considered prime. By the way, test-writers often include wrong answers designed to trap people who think 1 is a prime number.

Is 0 prime? No. For a number to be prime it must be divisible by itself. Division by zero is undefined, so 0 does not satisfy the definition of a prime number.

Can negative numbers be prime? Jeez, I was afraid you were going to ask this question. The short answer is that it depends on the mathematician you ask and what field they are researching. For our purposes, the better answer is that both the GMAT and GRE take the conventional approach of considering all primes to be positive.

We could go on asking questions about primes. Some of those questions would lead us into some fairly esoteric parts of math that are way, way, way beyond anything that you need to know for the GMAT or GRE!

The point of asking these questions, however, was to reinforce the idea that learning math concepts doesn't stop with making a flashcard and memorizing a definition or a formula. In many ways, learning math is like learning a language. When you study a language, you need to use the vocabulary and rules that you've memorized in all sorts of ways so that you can become comfortable with them. When you study math, you need to keep thinking about different situations in which the definitions, rules, and formulas can be used.

Keep the Pencil Nearby

As we've discussed, math is very much a learn-by-doing subject. Part of getting more comfortable with math is working through solutions on your own. While it may be tempting to simply read the explanations to problems in this book, you'll find that your comfort level with math will increase more quickly if you pick up a pencil and try the solution yourself!

There are several different ways that you can try the solution yourself. For any problem for which you think you understand the concept, try the solution yourself first. By doing so, you can compare your solution to the solution in the book. When you compare solutions, ask yourself questions such as "Did I skip any steps?" or "Did I make any unwarranted assumptions?" These questions help you to refine your approach.

For problems that you find more challenging, it's a good idea to follow along with the solution. Rather than just read the solution, grab a pencil and do the steps along with the solution. Some solutions may involve algebraic manipulations. You'll likely find that you understand these steps better if you write down the equation and do the step yourself rather than just trying to make sure that the step makes sense in your head.

For the hardest problems, you may need to read the solution first. In fact, you may even need to read the solution through a few times. Then, see if you can follow through the solution with your pencil in hand. To really make sure that you understand the solution, go back to the problem a few days later and try to solve it on your own before reading the solution.

One more thing about keeping the pencil handy. Most people find that the time allotted for the quantitative section(s) just evaporates. Blink and it's gone! As a result, many test-takers try save time by writing down as little as possible when solving a problem. However, that's actually a false time-saver. While you might save a couple of seconds on a couple of problems, you'll wind up wasting a lot of time if you need to rework a problem because the answer you got isn't one of the answer choices. Besides, thinking with your pencil is a great way to avoid the avoidable mistakes that put a serious dent in most people's scores.

Work with All Kinds of Numbers

One way that test-writers make problems harder is to have you do typical calculations using atypical numbers. For example, in the first chapter, we looked at some problems that made use of the formula for the area of a circle. As a quick reminder, the formula for the area of a circle is $A = \pi r^2$. In those problems, the radius of the circle was 4, a number that we use every day. We're comfortable with numbers such as 4, so it doesn't seem too hard to use the formula with a number such as 4.

But what if the radius of the circle had been a more unusual number, such as $\frac{1}{2}$, or $\sqrt{2}$, or $\frac{3}{\pi}$? Does that make using the formula to calculate the area of the circle more daunting? Many people would say that it does!

However, the first thing to realize is that while these numbers are more unusual, they are still numbers. Just as integers can be squared, these numbers can be squared. However, we do need to know a couple of special rules for squaring these numbers. For now, let's look at the quick version of those rules.

Let's handle the fractions first. Here's the rule: to square a fraction, square both the **numerator** (aka the top of the fraction) and the **denominator** (aka the bottom of the fraction). Here's the calculation when the radius is $\dfrac{1}{2}$.

$$A = \pi r^2 = \pi \left(\frac{1}{2}\right)^2 = \pi \left(\frac{1^2}{2^2}\right) = \pi \left(\frac{1}{4}\right) = \frac{\pi}{4}$$

Did you follow along with your pencil? If you did, that's great! If not, be sure to pick up your pencil for the next calculation.

Now, let's make the radius of the circle equal $\dfrac{3}{\pi}$. While the denominator of this fraction certainly looks unusual, there's no reason that the denominator can't be π. After all, π is just another number! Here's the calculation.

$$A = \pi r^2 = \pi \left(\frac{3}{\pi}\right)^2 = \pi \left(\frac{3^2}{\pi^2}\right) = \pi \left(\frac{9}{\pi^2}\right) = \frac{9\pi}{\pi^2} = \frac{9}{\pi}$$

Note that in the last step, we canceled the π in the numerator with one of the πs in the denominator.

Now, let's make the radius equal $\sqrt{2}$. Before we look at the calculation, we need to know how to square a square root. For now, we'll just give a quick synopsis of the *effect* of the rule. (Note that the effect of the rule is not quite the same thing as the rule. The rule itself is built on understanding why the rule works.) Here's the synopsis: to square a square root, remove the square root sign. Here's the calculation:

$$A = \pi r^2 = \pi \left(\sqrt{2}\right)^2 = \pi \left(2\right) = 2\pi$$

Now, here's why we did these calculations. When we discussed the need to do more than memorize, we discussed how you need to think about different applications of math terms so that you fully understand those terms. Using formulas with different types of numbers is one way that you can get comfortable with those formulas. In addition to using formulas with different types of numbers, you should also practice solving for the different parts of the formula. We just practiced solving for the area of a circle given different radii. The next step is to practice solving for the radius given different areas. I'll leave that exercise to you because we've also discussed that you need to do more than read this book to get ready for your test!

The First Step Is Enough to Get Started

As a test prep teacher and tutor, I've had a lot of experience watching people take math tests!

When you watch people doing a math problem, you'll notice two distinct approaches. Some people have their pencil in hand and are writing things down. Sometimes you'll see them scratch something out or erase a section of work. Then, they write something different down. Other people just sit and stare at the problem.

By the way, how often people just sit and stare at a problem is loosely correlated with the type of problem. People are more likely to try the problem when it is shorter than wordier. They are also most likely to try problems that test arithmetic concepts such as averages. They are most likely to sit and stare, lost in the fog of math, when the problem is testing a geometry concept. I guess there's just something about circles that makes people go round and round! Or, maybe there's something about triangles that makes people think that they'll never get to the point![2]

If you talk to the people who sit and stare at the problem, you'll hear a variety of explanations for this behavior. One of those explanations can be summarized as "I didn't know all the steps of the problem."

---

[2]   Bad jokes and math go together! I'll do my best to keep this instinct in check!

These people are experiencing FOGS, Fear of Getting Started. FOGS often afflicts people trying to solve math problems. Its symptoms include the pencil lying on the desk, scrunched up nose and forehead, and an almost dreamlike stare. People who experience FOGS are under the false impression that they need to know every step of the solution to a math problem before they start work.

However, I'm going to pass along a secret. People who are "good at math" usually don't know all the steps of the solution before they start work. Instead, they treat solving a math problem as an experiment. They usually have a good idea of how to start the problem and then they just figure the rest out as they go. The best way to find the second step of a solution is to write down the first step!

Moreover, people who are "good at math" aren't afraid to try things. Sometimes what they try leads to a dead end. Rather than getting frustrated, these people just try something else. In fact, they often view that dead end as a success. They gained some information about how to solve the problem by determining something that doesn't work!

So don't fall prey to FOGS! If you feel FOGS coming on when you look at a math problem, just remind yourself that there's no chance you'll solve the problem if you don't at least start the problem. If you think you know the first step, write it down and see where it leads! In the context of a standardized test such as the GMAT or the GRE, even a false start may allow you to eliminate an answer choice or two. That way, if you must guess, you've raised your odds of guessing correctly.

How Many Ways Can You Solve It?

Want a fun challenge when you study math?

When you study for your test, challenge yourself to find multiple ways to solve problems. Most math problems can be solved in more than one way. When you practice, it can be very helpful to work through multiple solutions. By doing so, you learn different ways to use the information in the problem. You also get more comfortable with the concepts tested by the problem.

Most importantly, you build flexibility into your approach. Really good standardized test-takers have two seemingly contradictory traits. On the one hand, they are very consistent in their approach. They have preferred tools for certain types of problems. In most cases, they will use their preferred tool to solve a problem of a certain type. However, sometimes they will find that their preferred tool doesn't work for a given problem. In those cases, those good standardized test-takers have built enough flexibility into their approach that they can reach for a different tool. Challenging yourself to solve problems in multiple ways is how you build a bigger toolbox so that you can build flexibility into your approach.

Let's give it a try.

Here's a sample problem. This problem is fairly straightforward. Both the GMAT and GRE would rate this problem as easy. After you read the problem, see whether you can come up with at least two ways to solve it before looking at the explanations.

A certain recipe requires $1\frac{1}{2}$ cups of sugar to make 3 dozen cookies. How many cups of sugar are required to make 1 dozen cookies using this recipe? (1 dozen = 12).

(A) $\frac{1}{3}$

(B) $\frac{1}{2}$

(C) 1

(D) 2

(E) $2\frac{1}{2}$

Did you come up with at least two solutions?

Seriously, if you didn't try to come up with at least two solutions, you're forgetting that we agreed that you need to do more than read! Pick up a pencil and give it a try! You can do this!

Okay, now let's compare notes.

Solution 1: Since we know the amount of sugar required to make three times the number of cookies that we want to make, we can just divide that amount of sugar by 3.

$$1\frac{1}{2} \div 3 = \frac{1}{2}$$

(If you are rusty working with mixed numbers, you can also think of this calculation as $1.5 \div 3 = 0.5$.)

Solution 2: If 1 dozen is 12 cookies, then 3 dozen is 36 cookies. We can divide $1\frac{1}{2}$ by 36 to find the amount of sugar needed to make one cookie. (But really, who would want to make only one cookie??)

$$1\frac{1}{2} \div 36 = \frac{3}{2} \div 36 = \frac{3}{2} \times \frac{1}{36} = \frac{3}{72} = \frac{1}{24}$$

Now that we know the amount of sugar needed to make 1 cookie,[3] we can multiply by 12 to find the amount needed to make 1 dozen cookies.

$$\frac{1}{24} \times 12 = \frac{12}{24} = \frac{1}{2}$$

Solution 3: We can use a proportion to solve. For now, we'll just note that proportions are used to scale a quantity up or down based on a known relationship.

Here, we'll set up the known relationship on the left of the equals sign and the relationship we want to find on the right of the equals sign.

$$\frac{1\frac{1}{2}\ cups}{3\ dozen} = \frac{x\ cups}{1\ dozen}$$

---

[3] Again, this calculation can be done using decimals: $1.5 \div 36 = 0.41\overline{6}$. Note, however, that the result is a repeating decimal which makes it messy. Moreover, the GMAT does not include a calculator, so being fraction-friendly is a real plus. Even for the GRE, there are times that fractions are better. We'll review working with fractions in an online bonus chapter.

We solve by cross-multiplying, an algebra technique used to solve an equation that consists of fractional expressions on both sides of an equals sign:

$$3x = 1\frac{1}{2}$$

Then divide both sides by 3 to find that $x = \frac{1}{2}$.

Did that last step remind you of anything? It's what we did for the first solution! Here's an example of how thinking about multiple solutions for a problem can help you to understand the concept better. The proportion approach helps us to understand why the first solution worked!

Can you figure out another way to set up the proportion? As a hint, think about the second solution.

Did you figure it out? Let's compare notes by looking at a fourth solution.

Solution 4: We'll use a different proportion to solve.

$$\frac{1\frac{1}{2}\ cups}{36\ cookies} = \frac{x\ cups}{12\ cookies}$$

Again, we'll cross-multiply.

$$36x = (12)\left(1\frac{1}{2}\right)$$

$$36x = (12)\left(\frac{3}{2}\right)$$

$$36x = 18$$

Divide both sides by 36 to find that $x = \frac{1}{2}$.

(Partial) Solution 5: There are a number of ways that math problems on standardized tests are different from those that were on tests that you took in school. One of the most significant differences is the inclusion of multiple-choice answer choices. The inclusion of these answer choices means that the person who wrote the problem had to solve the problem. In many cases, you can piggyback your work off that person's work.

Here, for example, we can ballpark. To be clear from the outset, ballparking isn't a solution strategy. That's why this solution is labeled as a partial solution. It won't get us to the answer. However, let's say that you were stuck. You can't figure out how to solve the problem. Alternatively, suppose that you were running short on time. Good standardized test-takers plan for these circumstances.

For this problem, we can think about the size of the answer. We know that it takes $1\frac{1}{2}$ cups of sugar to make 3 dozen cookies and we only want to make 1 dozen cookies. We'll definitely need less sugar. However, (D) and (E) suggest that we would need more sugar! Those can't be right so we can eliminate them. Now, if we are forced to guess, our odds of picking the correct answer are better.

Ballparking can't help us to decide between (A) and (B). That's why ballparking is rarely a solution strategy. It shouldn't be the first thing that you do. However, as you practice, you should practice making a guess when you run into a problem you don't know how to do before looking at the solution. One way to practice guessing is to look for any answers that are either too big or too small to be the correct answer.

Phew! That was quite a workout in terms of finding solutions for this problem! You may have even come up with some solutions that aren't listed here.

The overall point is that problem-solving can and should involve some creativity. You can't do things that aren't valid mathematically, but there is more than one way to solve most problems. Challenging yourself to find multiple solutions for at least one problem every time you practice will help you to understand math concepts better. In turn, that better understanding will help you to build flexibility into your problem-solving approach.

Learn from Mistakes

As you practice, you're going to make mistakes. That's normal. Even people who generally get very high scores on the GMAT or GRE make mistakes when practicing.

Mistakes are opportunities to learn. When you make a mistake on a practice problem, don't stop at reading the explanation. Going back to our earlier discussion, you need to do more than read the explanation. You also need to grab your pencil and work through the explanation. Then, you need to try the problem on your own. Try out other ways to solve the problem. Most importantly, go back to that problem that you got wrong a few days later and try to solve it again!

It's also a good idea to think about the causes of your mistakes. In some cases, you may discover that there are behaviors that are causing errors. For example, you may be reading the problem too quickly. Or, you may be skipping steps as you write out the work for the problem. You can train yourself to read the problem more slowly or to reread the problem before selecting your final answer. You can practice writing out your work more fully.

In other cases, you may discover that there's a concept that you don't understand. You can review the concept before trying other problems that test that concept.

Learning from your mistakes helps to reduce the number of errors that you make in the future.

Don't Get Frustrated

All of that brings us to one of the most important considerations when studying math: don't get frustrated!

Improvements take time. You'll likely find that some topics are easier to master than others. You may discover that one topic in particular is your personal kryptonite.

Keep at it!

When dealing with your personal kryptonite, start with easier problems. Work through the solutions. Then, try a problem that is a little harder. Celebrate your successes rather than dwelling on mistakes.

Don't give up! The goal is in sight!

Photo courtesy of John Fulmer

PART II

Let's Talk About Some Math

This section is not a comprehensive review of all the math you need to know for the GMAT or GRE. In fact, it's not even close!

This section will, however, introduce you to some of the important skills that constitute quantitative reasoning. In Section III, we'll discuss how those skills get tested in problems and see how knowledge of those skills can help solve problems.

For now, however, we're going to talk about some math. We're going to talk about some different types of numbers and the operations that can be performed with those numbers. We'll describe some of the connections among different types of numbers and how mathematicians think about numbers. We'll also try to demystify some of the language used when making mathematical statements. That will help with the wording that you'll encounter in GMAT and GRE problems.

We're also going to have some fun with the topic by telling a bit of a story and peppering in a little history. Along the way, we'll describe some of how these topics get used by the test-writers of the GMAT and GRE when constructing problems.

So, think of this section as an introduction to, and some examples of, quantitative reasoning. Hopefully, this section will help inform how you think about math as you prepare for the GMAT or GRE. Math is more than formulas and definitions, and formulas and definitions will only get you so far on either the GMAT or GRE. To excel on either test, you also need to work on the quantitative reasoning aspect of that particular test.

Let's get to it!

CHAPTER 3

Number Systems

We are about to embark on another ahistorical journey! Buckle up!

Some of humanity's earliest math problems involved working with numbers. Consider our ancestors in the Paleolithic Era.[1] Let's say that you want to make a spear with a stone head. You'll need some concept of weight. After all, if the stone is too heavy, you won't be able to hurl the spear as far. If the stone is too light, it won't penetrate whatever you are hunting deeply enough. You'll also need to consider the shape of the stone. How thick is the right stone? How long?

Once you are out on the hunt, you'll need some form of organization for you and your fellow hunters. Who throws the spear first? Who throws second? How do you designate that? How do you describe the number of hunters with you?

Let's say that gathering is more your thing. You've been sent out to collect berries for your band. How many do you need?[2] How do you divide up what you've gathered once you have met up with the rest of your band?

I'm not suggesting that our Paleolithic ancestors engaged in complicated mathematical exercises to answer these questions. Many of these questions can be answered intuitively or through experience. But still, you can see the need for a rudimentary form of mathematics developing.

Natural Numbers

The rudimentary form of mathematics starts with the concept of natural numbers. **Natural numbers** are just the counting numbers with one addition. That one addition is the number zero. So, the natural numbers are 0, 1, 2, 3, 4....[3]

---

[1] Middle to Upper Paleolithic, to be precise.
[2] The simple answer may be: as many as you can carry!
[3] There are lots of sets and lists in math that never end. These sets are described as infinite. Infinity is a big deal in mathematics. There are even levels to infinity. Yes, one infinite set can be "bigger" than another! We don't need to know or understand too much about infinity for our purposes. That's why this text is in a footnote!

Whether zero is a natural number is actually the subject of a long-standing mathematical and philosophical debate. You may have even read about how some ancient Greek philosophers got all twisted up in their contemplation of zero by asking, "How can not being be?" Still, most mathematicians consider zero a natural number and we'll follow suit.[4]

Note that the natural numbers are some of the first numbers that you learn as a child. Of course, if you ask most young children to count to ten, they'll probably start with 1 rather than 0.[5] So, here's the first instance where you may need to undo an old habit. The natural numbers start with zero!

Now that we've defined the natural numbers, let's get an idea of what we can do with them. Back to our prehistoric ancestors and some of the problems with which they had to contend.

Humans are a naturally acquisitive lot. If you have two berries, you're probably going to want a third berry! More to the point, somewhere along the way, our ancestors started to notice that if you already had two berries and added, say, three berries to your stash of berries, you always ended up with five berries. Thus, addition was born![6] You'd also eventually notice that if you started off with three berries and add two berries, you also always wind up with five berries. So, the order in which you add numbers doesn't matter. Rules are starting to be discovered!

There's more! Our ancestors eventually would have realized that if you started out with one berry and added four berries, you also wind up with five berries. In other words, there are different groups of numbers that you can add together to achieve a given result. Addition is powerful stuff!

---

[4] Mathematics, for all its rigor, does sometimes bow to expediency. Sometimes problematic questions such as "Is zero a natural number?" are decided by nothing other than which answer leads to better results. We'll refer to such definitions as Dead Mathematician Rules. Why is zero a natural number? Some dead mathematician said so!

[5] If the child responds 0, 1, 2, 3..., that child probably has at least one parent who is a mathematician!

[6] Really, the discovery of addition was likely a long process that involved a lot of development of the concept of numbers and the concomitant development of language. But remember, this is an ahistorical journey that we're on! We're only interested in the broad contours as a way of helping us to see how some of the parts of mathematics fit together.

Negative Numbers

Of course, there were other practical problems that our ancestors had to solve. Once you've gathered some berries, you might also start to notice that there are rules for how many berries remain once you've eaten a given number of berries. In other words, if you start with ten berries and eat two berries (because, you know, hunger), you always wind up with eight berries. So, just as you can add with natural numbers, you can also subtract with natural numbers.

However, there's a key difference. The order in which you add natural numbers doesn't matter. But the order in which you subtract natural numbers *does* matter. You can subtract three from eight. From our ancestors' point of view, subtracting eight from three made no sense. How could you wind up with less than nothing? After all, you can't count negative berries.

For that reason, it took a very long time to develop the concept of negative numbers. Greek mathematicians of the Hellenistic period mostly ignored negative solutions to the problems with which they were concerned. The first reference to and use of negative numbers comes from a Chinese text compiled by several generations of scholars between the 10th and 2nd centuries BCE. Mathematicians in India also eventually started using negative numbers.

One of the earliest uses of negative numbers was to denote debts. See! Math once again solving a real-world problem! Not only are humans acquisitive by nature, we're used to owing other people things, whether those things be favors, money, or berries.

A bit more seriously, while we've compressed the timeline of the development of negative numbers quite a bit, we needed to introduce them so that we could move beyond the natural numbers. While the natural numbers can be used to solve many mathematical problems, the use of subtraction, one of the basic operations on numbers, shows that we need more types of numbers than just the natural numbers.

Enter integers. **Integers** add negative whole numbers to the natural numbers. We can engage in a bit of quantitative reasoning by constructing the integers from the natural numbers. Take each of the whole numbers greater than 0 and subtract that number from 0. If you do this methodically, which is a core attribute of quantitative reasoning, you can derive each of the negative numbers. In other words, perform the operations: $0 - 1 = -1$; $0 - 2 = -2$; $0 - 3 = -3$; etc.

We now have a more robust system of numbers with which to work. With the integers, we can both add and subtract and always get a result. Integers solve the problem that we encountered with subtraction when working with only the natural numbers. We now have a way to subtract a larger number from a smaller number.

But, we need to expand our universe of numbers even more.

Fractions

Let's check in on our Paleolithic ancestors again. They've got another math problem to solve. The gatherers have returned with the berries and it's time to start distributing the berries. We'll assume for the moment that everyone in the band is supposed to get an equal share.

Sometimes the distribution process is going to work out okay. Let's say that the band consists of 10 members, and you've collected 30 berries that you need to hand out. You start by giving everyone one berry, then a second berry, and then a third. You are now out of berries, and everyone is happy. No one feels cheated.

However, one day you pick 32 berries and now you have a problem with distributing the berries. You can't divide the berries so that everyone gets an equal share. There are two mathematical solutions to that problem.[7]

One way to solve this problem works with either natural numbers or integers. In this case, if you collect 32 berries that you are trying to evenly distribute to 10 people, you simply have two berries left. Maybe you keep them until the next day. But hey, we've just seen the invention of the remainder, an important concept in integer division.

---

[7] There are also some non-mathematical solutions to the problem. Those include an unequal distribution in which one or more members of the band are considered special and, therefore, deserving of a larger share. Or, you could just decide to leave those two berries on the bush when you are out gathering but that, too, is a mathematical solution!

The alternative is to expand the universe of numbers again. Once you've handed out 3 berries to each of the 10 people in your band, you could split the remaining 2 berries evenly.[8] In this case, each person would also get an additional one-fifth of a berry.

Our universe of numbers has now expanded to include **fractions**. The type of numbers that we are now considering are the rational numbers. **Rational numbers** are any numbers that can be expressed as a fraction where the top number (aka the numerator) is an integer, and the bottom number (aka the denominator) is a **nonzero integer**. The rational numbers include the integers and all positive or negative fractions, including **improper fractions**.[9]

Fractions have been around for a long time. The ancient Egyptians, Sumerians, Babylonians, and Greeks all used some version of fractions. That's not surprising, as fractions solve the problem of dividing a whole unit of something among two or more people. Or put another way, two people somewhere solved the problem of having only one berry by cutting it in half! The earliest fractions were, in fact, **unit fractions**. Unit fractions are fractions for which the numerator is 1 and the denominator is an integer greater than 0. These fractions can be easily formed by the natural numbers.

Our story of numbers is almost complete. We have arrived at the rational numbers on which we can perform the four basic operations:

- Addition
- Subtraction
- Multiplication
- Division

Note, however, that division still presents one problem for the rational numbers. For addition, subtraction, and multiplication, you can take any two rational numbers, perform the operation, and get a rational number as the result.

---

[8] Of course, your knife may not be equal to the task!

[9] Improper fractions are fractions for which the top number (aka the numerator) is greater than the bottom number (aka the denominator). For example, $\frac{5}{2}$ is an improper fraction and hence a rational number.

Let's see whether you can figure out the problem for division with rational numbers before reading the next paragraph.

No, seriously, see if you can figure it out first! We've delayed the paragraph with the answer to give you time to consider the problem. Remember that asking questions about numbers is part of quantitative reasoning!

Did you say if one or both of the rational numbers is zero? If so, you've got it! You can divide zero by any other rational number to get a result of zero, which is a rational number. However, you cannot divide by zero. Nor can you divide zero by zero. Division by zero is considered *undefined*. In other words, $0 \div 2 = 0$ and is a valid statement in mathematics. However, $2 \div 0$ is not a valid statement. In GMAT and GRE problems, you'll often see a statement such as $x \neq 0$ to rule out the possibility of dividing by zero.[10]

The problem with dividing by zero doesn't cause us to expand our universe of numbers. However, we do still have one issue to consider that will require us to expand our universe of numbers. In doing so, we'll arrive at the type of numbers that are used in most math problems on the GMAT and GRE.

Real Numbers

Once ways to write different types of numbers were developed,[11] it became possible to study numbers. Mathematicians in all the great ancient civilizations studied numbers. In some cases, they were trying to solve practical problems. However, math had progressed far enough by this point that some study of numbers was done simply to discover new results about numbers.

---

[10] Such statements can be considered technical requirements of the problem. If the test-writers didn't specifically rule out division by zero in certain problems, a test-taker could reasonably claim that the problem is invalid and cannot be answered. That's a test-writer's worst nightmare! They aren't about to let that happen!

[11] Those ways looked nothing like how we write numbers today!

Let's go look over the shoulder of Hippasus of Metapontum,[12] a Greek mathematician of the Pythagorean school who lived around 530 BCE to 450 BCE. He's about to make a remarkable discovery.[13]

One day, Hippasus is studying a **right triangle**. In this triangle, the two sides that form the 90° angle have equal lengths, and those lengths are integers.[14] From the **Pythagorean Theorem**,[15] he knows that the length of the **hypotenuse** is not an integer. He's trying to find a common unit of measurement between the length of one of the sides and the length of the hypotenuse. Think of it as if he's got a ruler and he's trying to find a unit of measurement to divide up the ruler so that he can say something like "The **leg** is 5 of these marks and the hypotenuse is 7 of these marks." It's important to him that he only count a full number of marks on the ruler. So, he won't be satisfied with 5.5 marks for the leg and 7 marks for the hypotenuse.

He finds that no such unit of measurement exists. Not only does he find that no such unit of measurement exists, he proves that it doesn't exist.

That may not sound like a big deal, but he's just discovered irrational numbers. An **irrational number** is a number that cannot be expressed as a fraction $\frac{a}{b}$, where a is an integer and b is a nonzero integer. More specifically, if the legs of the triangle have a length of 1, he's just proven that $\sqrt{2}$ is an irrational number.[16] If $\sqrt{2}$ is irrational, it means that there is no fraction $\frac{a}{b}$ that, when multiplied by itself, produces 2 as the product. The square root of any integer that is not a **perfect square**[17] is also an irrational number. There are also other irrational numbers. One of the most famous, and one that appears on both the GMAT and GRE, is π.

---

[12] As is often the case with ancient discoveries, there is some debate over whether Hippasus actually made the discovery that we are about to credit him with.

[13] Unfortunately, if some of the earlier accounts are correct, this discovery cost him his life.

[14] This triangle is an **isosceles right triangle**, which is sometimes referred to as a 45-45-90 triangle.

[15] The Pythagorean Theorem describes the relationships between the sides of a right triangle. The relationship is given by $a^2 + b^2 = c^2$, where a and b are the legs of the triangle and c is the hypotenuse.

[16] The square root of a number is a number that, when multiplied by itself, produces the number under the radical. For example, $\sqrt{9}$ is 3 because $3 \times 3 = 9$.

[17] Perfect squares are integers such as 4 that have integer square roots.

Now that we've introduced irrational numbers, we're ready to discuss one more type of number. If you combine all the irrational numbers and all the rational numbers, you have a set of numbers called the **real numbers**. Real numbers are important for our purposes. Both the GMAT and the GRE construct problems for which the answer and the numbers that you use to solve those problems are real numbers.

Sometimes the GMAT and GRE test-writers will put constraints on problems. For example, a problem may state that a variable can only be an integer. Or, a problem may state that a variable is a positive number. However, in all cases, the problems use real numbers.[18]

As we've expanded our universe of numbers, we've been building a hierarchy in which one set of numbers is typically a subset of another set of numbers. In other words:

- All natural numbers are also integers.
- All integers are also rational numbers.
- All rational numbers are real numbers.
- A natural number is also an integer, a rational number, and a real number.
- An integer is also a rational number and a real number.
- We can't go in the other direction: not all integers are natural numbers.

Now that you know all that, ask yourself a few questions:

- Can you give some examples of integers that aren't natural numbers?
- How about examples of rational numbers that aren't integers?
- What about some examples of real numbers that aren't rational numbers?

---

[18]   Yes, there are other types of numbers. You may remember complex numbers from school. There are even more exotic types of numbers with equally exotic names such as surreal and hyperreal numbers. Fortunately, the GMAT and GRE confine themselves to real numbers!

As discussed in the How to Study Math chapter, you should ask yourself these types of questions to ensure your understanding of concepts. If you didn't try to answer the questions, you've got one more chance to do so! Okay, this footnote provides some answers to the first two questions.[19]

As for the third question, the answer to that requires more than a footnote. An irrational number is a real number that is not a rational number. So, if you answered something such as $\sqrt{2}$ to the third question, that's great! However, note that irrational numbers break up our hierarchy of numbers. So, we can say that all natural numbers are also integers, rational numbers, and real numbers. We can also say that all irrational numbers are also real numbers. However, we CANNOT say that any natural number or rational number is an irrational number.

Why have we spent so much time describing different types of numbers?

Well, there are two reasons. First, as stated, math problems on the GMAT and GRE use real numbers, so you need to know what a real number is. The second reason is perhaps the more important for our purposes. Considering different cases is a core aspect of mathematical reasoning. Both the GMAT and GRE include problems that require you to think through whether a rule or expression applies for all numbers or only certain types of numbers. So, it becomes important to understand when a rule applies and when it doesn't.

Relational Operators

There are two more properties of numbers that we need to discuss. Let's go back to the natural numbers for a moment. Our prehistoric ancestors would have noticed that 2 berries are more than 1 berry. They would have also noticed that 3 berries are more than both 2 berries and 1 berry. Eventually, someone would have noticed that since 5 berries are more than 4 berries and 4 berries are more than 3 berries, then 5 berries must be more than 3 berries. This property is referred to as **transitivity**.

---

[19] Any negative whole number is an integer but not a natural number. So, if you said something such as −2 to answer the first question, good job! Any proper fraction is a rational number that isn't an integer. So, if you said something such as $\frac{1}{2}$ to answer the second question, you've got it!

Transitivity

Transitivity is actually a property of **relational operators** rather than numbers. What does that mean? Let's consider a real-world example before we turn to math. If you know that Ben is a descendant of Charlie and that Charlie is a descendant of Jack, what do you know about Ben's relationship to Jack? Yes, you know that Ben is also Jack's descendant. That means that the "descendant of" relationship is transitive. Here, we could call "descendant of," a relational operator because it expresses a relationship between two items. Not all relational operators are transitive. For example, let's change our scenario just a bit to say that Jack is the father of Charlie and Charlie is the father of Ben. Now, our relational operator is "father of," and this relational operator is not transitive because Jack is not Ben's father.

Okay, back to math. There are five common relational operators that are used on the GMAT and GRE. This table shows these five operators.

Operator	Notation
Equal to	=
Greater than	>
Greater than or equal to	≥
Less than	<
Less than or equal to	≤

Each of these five relational operators is transitive. For example, if a problem states that $x = y$ and $y = z$, then $x = z$ follows from the transitive property for the *equal to* operator. Similarly, a problem may state that $x > y > z$ and that means $x > z$. These sorts of statements place constraints on the numbers that can be used in problems. It's often helpful to think about examples when solving problems. If the problem states that $x > y > z$, then $x = 4$, $y = 3$, and $z = 2$ is a good example but $x = 4$, $y = 3$, $z = 3$ is not because it violates that condition in the problem. It's important that examples satisfy any conditions in the problem. Otherwise, errors ensue.

These relational operators work on all real numbers. Put another way, for any two real numbers, two numbers are either equal or one number is greater than the other. Both the GMAT and the GRE feature problems for which it's important to keep that basic fact about numbers in mind!

Here's a more formal statement of transitivity using the *greater than* relational operator as an example. Similar statements could be given for each of the other four relational operators.

For all x, y, and z, where x, y, and z are real numbers,

if x > y > z, then x > z.

Well-Order

Let's go back to the natural numbers for a moment and explore the statement that, for real numbers, two numbers are either equal or one number is greater than the other. Natural numbers are also real numbers so this statement applies. However, there's more to the story for natural numbers and that brings us to the second property of numbers that we want to consider. Natural numbers comprise a set of numbers that mathematicians would call **well-ordered**.[20] Natural numbers have both a least element and successor elements. For natural numbers, the least element is 0. For each natural number, the next natural number can be found by adding 1. In other words, you can count with the natural numbers. For example, from 5, you can find the next number (the successor) by adding 1 and you can find the previous number (the predecessor) by subtracting 1.

Most of the types of numbers that are used in GMAT and GRE problems lack one or both of these properties. Each integer has a predecessor and a successor. However, there's no least integer. Because integers have predecessor and successor integers, you can answer questions such as "What is the greatest integer that is less than −3?"[21]

---

[20] Here's another instance where the concept is important, but the term isn't, as neither the GMAT nor the GRE uses the term *well-ordered.*

[21] It's −4. Statements such as this are often used in GMAT and GRE problems. It's best to parse the language one step at a time. First, think about all the integers that are less than −3. So, we want integers that are further away from 0 than −3. There's an infinite number of such numbers, but we can list out just a few of the integers. We'll list them in ascending order: ... −6, −5, −4. We want the greatest of those integers, and that is −4.

Once we enter the realm of rational, irrational, and real numbers, however, there are no predecessor or successor numbers. There are, of course, numbers that are greater or less than any given number. There just isn't a next one. For example, what's the next rational number greater than $\frac{1}{2}$?[22] For any two different real numbers, we can always find another real number in between, no matter how close together the two numbers are.

That means that it's important to pay attention to the types of numbers allowed for any given problem. For example, if a problem states that $x > 5$, the meaning of that statement changes if x is an integer rather than a real number. If x is an integer, we know that the minimum value of x is 6. However, if x is a real number, then there is no minimum value. So, it's important to pay attention to the wording. Did the problem start by starting "If x is an integer and $x > 5$..." or "If $x > 5$...." The second statement implies that x is a real number because all numbers on both the GMAT and GRE are real numbers unless language in the question states that you should only consider a certain type of real number, such as an integer.

For real numbers, statements such as $x > 4$ or $x < 10$ are stating either a **lower bound** ($x > 4$) or an **upper bound** ($x < 10$) for the real numbers that should be considered when solving the problem. For the statement $x > 4$, 4 is considered the lower bound. Values for x can get really close to 4 but cannot actually reach or equal 4.[23] For the statement $x < 10$, 10 is considered the upper bound. Values for x can get really close to 10 but cannot actually reach or equal 10. For example, it might be important to realize that x could be 10.01 or 10.001 in a problem that includes this statement.

---

[22] Be careful! It's not $\frac{1}{3}$! While $\frac{1}{3}$ is less than $\frac{1}{2}$, note that $\frac{1}{3}$ is not the predecessor of $\frac{1}{2}$ because we can always find another rational number, such as $\frac{3}{10}$, which lies between $\frac{1}{3}$ and $\frac{1}{2}$.

[23] The mathy terminology here is that the values of x can get arbitrarily close to 4.

It should also be noted that in a statement such as $x \geq 4$, 4 is also the lower bound. In this case, however, the value of x can be 4. So, it's important to pay attention to which relational operator is used! When a problem includes a condition such as $x \geq 4$ there are generally fewer opportunities for test-takers to make mistakes. For these problems, it's important to consider what happens when $x = 4$, but it's usually not important to consider what happens when x equals a number close to 4, such as $x = 4.01$.

You may also see problems that include statements that provide both lower and upper bounds. For example, $4 < x < 10$ means that 4 is the lower bound and 10 is the upper bound for the values of x. For such statements, it's very important to note whether the problem states that x is an integer. If x is an integer, then the only possible values of x are 5, 6, 7, 8, and 9. However, if the problem doesn't state that x is an integer, then any value of x between 4 and 10 is permitted. For example, x could be an integer such as 5 or a non-integer such as 4.01, 7.5, or 9.99. One common mistake that test-takers make is to look at a statement such as $4 < x < 10$ and assume that x is an integer and so can only take on 5 values. If the question didn't state that x is an integer, that's a bad assumption! As discussed earlier, the test-writers like to take advantage of bad assumptions when constructing answer choices.

Now, let's get to work reviewing the basic operations that can be performed with numbers and the properties of different types of numbers. We'll start with basic operations.

CHAPTER 4

Basic Operations with Numbers

There are six basic operations with numbers that both the GMAT and the GRE expect you to understand and be able to use. Those six operations are: addition, subtraction, multiplication, division, raising a number to a power (aka exponentiation), and taking a root of a number. For both the GMAT and the GRE, taking the root of a number usually means taking either the square root or the cube root.

Note that being able to use an operation is a little different from understanding the operation. For example, knowing how to add two numbers, such as two integers or two fractions, means that you can use the operation of addition. In other words, you know and can use an algorithm to produce a sum. Knowing that the sum of two negative numbers yields a negative number means that you understand a property of that operation for certain kinds of numbers. While you probably know how to use the basic operations, you may not have thought too much about their properties.

In this section, we're going to mostly discuss the important[1] properties of addition, subtraction, multiplication, and division. We'll also briefly touch upon exponentiation and roots, but a more thorough review of the properties of these operations would also require a more thorough review of the rules for using these operations.[2]

Whenever possible, we'll illustrate the properties using integers as our examples so that we can pay more attention to the properties of the operations than to the mechanics of the operation. After all, most people are more comfortable performing addition with 2 and 7 than with $\frac{1}{2}$ and $\frac{2}{3}$. It's also true that both the GMAT and GRE are less interested in your calculating ability[3] than in your ability to reason with mathematical concepts. That means that understanding properties of even well-known operations, such as addition, is important to getting a great score!

Before we start discussing the properties of the basic operations, let's go over two quick things to keep in mind.

---

[1] For our purposes, "important" means that the GMAT and GRE expect you to know about these properties!

[2] For that more thorough review, check out the bonus chapter in your online Student Tools.

[3] If the GRE cared about your calculating ability, they wouldn't provide an on-screen calculator. Both tests mostly choose numbers for the problems that make the calculations work out nicely.

First, as discussed in Chapter 3, integers are whole numbers that can be positive, negative, or, in the case of zero, neither positive nor negative. So, the integers are ... –2, –1, 0, 1, 2 ....

Second, we need this definition for real numbers.

All real numbers, including integers, can be classified as

- Positive, if the number is greater than zero
- Negative, if the number is less than zero
- Neither positive nor negative, in the case of zero. Zero is the only real number that is neither positive nor negative. Because zero is an integer, zero is also the only integer that is neither positive nor negative.

Four of our six basic operations always yield an integer as a result when performed on integers. Which of the six operations can yield a result that is not an integer when performed with integers? Have you got your answer? The correct answer can be found in this footnote.[4]

We'll start our discussion by looking at the four operations that always produce an integer when performed on integers. In that way, we can keep our examples straightforward as we learn to think about the properties of operations.

Addition

First up, let's talk about addition.

As discussed earlier, addition is likely one of the first operations that our distant ancestors performed with numbers. **Addition** was first performed with natural numbers. As the concept of numbers evolved to include integers, it became possible to work out some rules for addition with integers. Many of those rules can also be applied to addition with real numbers. We'll state the rules first for addition with integers; then we'll state a more general version of these rules.[5]

---

[4] Division with two integers may not produce an integer as a result. For example, $5 \div 2$ does not yield an integer. Taking the square root of an integer is the other operation that may not result in an integer. For example, $\sqrt{3}$ does not yield an integer.

[5] Starting with a less general case is a standard practice in mathematics. The less general case is usually more straightforward, and that helps to get a handle on the basics.

Here are some basic rules for addition with integers:

- The sum of two positive integers is a positive integer.
- The sum of two negative integers is a negative integer.
- The sum of a positive integer and a negative integer can be either a positive integer, a negative integer, or zero, which is an integer that is neither positive nor negative.
- For each positive integer, a, there exists a negative integer, b, for which the sum of a and b is zero. $(a + b = 0)$
- The sum of any integer, a, and zero is a. $(a + 0 = a)$
- The order in which two integers are added does not change the sum.
- The order in which three or more integers are added does not change the sum.

Who knew there were so many rules for addition, right? In fact, we could state more rules, but let's use the rules above to engage in some quantitative reasoning. As we've discussed, both the GMAT and the GRE like to test how thoroughly you understand basic rules. So, let's use these basic rules as a starting point to see what else we know about addition with integers. After all, the ability to generalize is one of the core elements of quantitative reasoning.

Sum of Two Positive Integers

Let's start with the first rule. Remember that we said that it's necessary to do more than memorize a rule to understand it? Examples are good ways to start thinking about rules because examples help us to figure out what rules mean and how those rules can be applied. So, let's come up with an example. We can start with $2 + 5 = 7$. That seems pretty straightforward. Notice, however, that the rule didn't state that the two integers had to be different. So, we could also have used $2 + 2 = 4$ as our example. Next, we can notice that in each of our examples, the sum was greater than either of the two integers we added together.

Let's make the rule sound more like the rule that you might encounter in a math text:

The sum of a and b, where a and b are positive integers, is a positive integer, c, where $c > a$ and $c > b$.

Now our simple rule about adding two positive integers—a rule that we've all known since grade school—sounds a lot more complicated, doesn't it? Math is actually full of relatively simple ideas that someone decided to make sound as complicated as possible! That math rules (and problems!) often sound complicated is the result of the precise use of language in math. It can take some effort to unpack the language, but as you study, you will get more comfortable with the language. Thinking about examples and solving problems are two ways to get more comfortable with the math language that you'll encounter in preparing for and taking the GMAT or GRE.

Sum of Two Negative Integers

Let's tackle the second rule. This time, we'll start with the way that rule might sound in a math text.[6]

The sum of a and b, where a and b are negative integers, is a negative integer, c, where $c < a$ and $c < b$.

Let's think about this statement by using some examples. First, $-2 + -5 = -7$. Okay, that example helps us to understand the statement. We took two negative integers, -2 and -5, and found their sum, -7. Then, note that $-7 < -2$ and $-7 < -5$.[7] Now, since we're paying careful attention to the wording, we notice that we aren't required to choose two different numbers. So, let's try an example where the two negative integers are the same: $-2 + -2 = -4$. Again, everything checks out. We took the sum of two negative integers, got a negative result, and note that $-4 < -2$.

Now, let's see whether we can expand upon those first two rules. Professional mathematicians are always in search of a more general solution or rule. In fact, generalization is one of the driving forces in the study of mathematics. While the GMAT and GRE won't explicitly test your ability to generalize in a strict mathematical sense, both tests do penalize test-takers who are wont to make bad assumptions. In many cases, those bad assumptions are based on attempts to apply a rule in a situation where it doesn't apply. In other words, some bad

---

[6] From now on, we'll use the term *mathy* to describe such language!

[7] As a reminder, negative numbers get smaller the further away from zero they are.

assumptions are based on an attempt to overgeneralize. Test-writers often construct wrong answers based on the bad assumptions they expect test-takers to make.

Moreover, both tests sometimes write problems that are based on generalizations of more familiar rules. For example, you may recall this rule that defines multiplication with square roots: $\sqrt{ab} = \sqrt{a} \times \sqrt{b}$. This same rule generalizes to other types of roots, such as cube roots. Most people studying to take the GMAT or GRE only study the form of the rule stated above. Here's what the rule looks like for cube roots: $\sqrt[3]{ab} = \sqrt[3]{a} \times \sqrt[3]{b}$. If you were a savvy test-writer who was tasked with writing a harder problem, you might test the rule for cube roots rather than square roots. When you work with a rule, it's always helpful to ask whether there is a more general form!

At any rate,[8] let's get back to our first two rules for addition. Note that we phrased both rules in terms of two numbers. Do we need to limit ourselves to two numbers? Of course not! If we take the sum of three positive numbers, the sum is a positive number that is greater than any of the three positive numbers that were added to produce the sum. And, if we can do that with three positive integers, then we can do that same thing with four positive integers, and we can just keep going. The same logic (and generalization) applies to sums of negative integers.

Sum of a Positive and a Negative Integer

Now, let's tackle the next two rules together because they are related. Some math rules are extensions of other rules. So far, we've considered addition involving only positive numbers or only negative numbers and gotten nice results. However, if we consider addition of one positive and one negative integer, our results become more complicated. For example,[9] $-2 + 5 = 3$, so we can add a positive integer and a negative integer and get a positive integer as the result. However, $-4 + 2 = -2$, so we can also get a negative integer as the result. Moreover, we can also get zero as the sum. For example, $-3 + 3 = 0$.

While we could state some additional rules to clarify the possible outcomes when adding a positive and a negative integer, we don't want

---

[8] Except faster than the speed of light, as one of my friends from college would always interject when I would use that phrase. Physicists!

[9] More examples! Examples are an important tool for thinking about and learning math!

to go overboard with rules. What's more important for our purposes is the reasoning strategy that we're employing. One aspect of quantitative reasoning that gets tested on the GMAT and the GRE is the ability to consider different cases. As previously discussed, evaluating different cases helps us to avoid making bad assumptions (and hence mistakes!) when solving problems.

There's one other part of our discussion about adding one positive and one negative integer that is noteworthy. We stated that the result can be zero. Our fourth rule states that for each positive integer, there exists a negative integer that we can add to that positive integer to obtain a sum of zero. For example, we can add –3 to 3 to get zero: –3 + 3 = 0.

Additive Inverses

Pairs of numbers such as –3 and 3 are called **additive inverses**. While it's nice to know the proper math term, neither the GMAT nor the GRE uses the term additive inverse. However, the concept is important for a few reasons. First, inverses are important to your understanding of math and hence to your quantitative reasoning ability. Real-world math often involves operations that undo each other. For example, if you go shopping and add 3 oranges to your cart, taking 3 oranges out of your cart undoes the addition of the oranges. Thus, addition and subtraction can be thought of as **inverse operations**. One undoes the effects of the other. The same can be said of multiplication and division. If you multiply by 2 and then divide by 2, you wind up where you started. Solving many types of equations involves using inverse operations.

Second, we can use the concept of additive inverses to introduce both a key math concept and a key component of quantitative reasoning. Notice that the reason that –3 and 3 sum to 0 (or cancel each other out) is that they are equally spaced around zero. That observation introduces two concepts. The first is symmetry, which is a core aspect of mathematical (and quantitative) reasoning. The solutions to some GMAT and GRE problems involve noticing and using symmetry.

Now we can introduce a key math concept. We've been discussing additive inverses in a rather informal way. Suppose we wanted to state the definition more formally, just as we've done with some of our other rules.

Here's one way to do that:

Two real numbers,[10] a and b, are additive inverses if $a + b = 0$.

However, let's go back to that language about the numbers being equally spaced around zero. Another way to state that idea is to say that -3 and 3 are the same distance from zero on the number line. When we start discussing the distance that a number is from zero on the number line, we are referring to that number's absolute value. The **absolute value** of a real number is the distance that the number is from zero on the number line.

Before we state our definition of additive inverses using absolute values, let's go over a couple of things to know about absolute values. First, absolute value is indicated by a pair of parallel bars around a number or an expression. For example, $|3|$ indicates that you need to find the absolute value of 3. Next, absolute values are always **nonnegative**. So, $|3| = 3$ and $|-3| = 3$ because both 3 and -3 are a distance of 3 from 0 on the number line. Finally, note that $|0| = 0$. This last example is the reason that we said that absolute values are always nonnegative rather than positive. There's no reason to exclude the possibility of taking the absolute value of 0.

Now we are ready to state the definition of additive inverses using absolute values:

Two real numbers, a and b, where $a \neq b$, are additive

inverses if $|a| = |b|$.

---

[10] Remember that we said that some of the definitions that apply to integers also apply to all real numbers rather than just to the integers. This is one of those definitions.

Identity Element for Addition

Now that we've discussed additive inverses, it's time to discuss the identity element for addition. That brings us to our fifth rule. For addition (and subtraction), zero is referred to as the **identity element**. Again, that's the mathy term, and neither the GMAT nor GRE uses the term identity element. However, the concept is important.

So, what do we mean when we say that zero is the identity element for addition? Consider what happens when we add zero to a number. For example, 4 + 0 = 4. We're right back where we started, aren't we? Adding zero produced a sum that was equal to the number to which we added zero. So, an identity element is just a number that, when we use it in an operation, leaves some other number that we used in that operation unchanged.

Why does that matter? Again, it goes to the idea that the GMAT and GRE test-writers try to get us to make false assumptions and ignore special cases. If you were to ask most people for a definition of addition, the response would probably be something along the lines of "it's something done to make something bigger." But, that's not always the case. The result depends on the numbers that you add. One of the possibilities is that the result, or sum, is equal to one of the numbers that are added.[11] Remembering that identity elements exist for some operations helps us to consider all the special cases that we need when picking an answer. We'll have more to say about considering cases as an aspect of quantitative reasoning as our math journey unfolds.

Commutative and Associative Properties

Finally, let's discuss the last two rules. The sixth rule says that the order in which we add two integers doesn't matter. Again, we'll start with an example: 2 + 5 = 5 + 2. Phrased more generally, we could state the rule like this:

For all a and b, where a and b are integers, $a + b = b + a$.

---

[11] Just for fun, the term for the numbers that are added to produce a sum is addends. Yes, math has a word for everything!

This property is called the **commutative property** for addition. It's important that we state the operation when discussing the commutative property. That's because some operations are commutative, and some are not. Addition and multiplication are commutative, but subtraction and division are not.

The commutative property is stated in terms of two numbers. What if there are more than two numbers? Again, think in terms of an example. Does $2 + 3 + 4 = 3 + 4 + 2$? It does! This property is referred to as the **associative property** for addition. Like the commutative property, the associative property holds for addition and multiplication, but not for subtraction or division.

Phrased more generally, we could state the associative property for addition like this:

For all a, b, and c, where a, b, and c are integers, $(a + b) + c = a + (b + c)$.[12]

Addition of Real Numbers

Of course, addition can be performed with numbers beyond just the integers. In fact, addition can be performed with any type of real numbers. We'll close our discussion of addition by restating our rules for addition in terms of real numbers rather than just integers. We'll also incorporate some of the other things we discovered about these rules.

Here are the rules for addition with real numbers.[13]

- The sum of a and b, where a and b are positive real numbers, is a positive real number, c, where $c > a$ and $c > b$.
- The sum of a and b, where a and b are negative real numbers, is a negative real number, c, where $c < a$ and $c < b$.

---

[12] Here the notation is making use of the **order of operations**, which dictates that operations enclosed in parentheses are completed first. We'll have more to say about the order of operations in a few pages.

[13] We've stated these rules in the mathy way! We've built up to using the mathy language so now is the time to use it!

- The sum of a positive real number and a negative real number can be either a positive real number, a negative real number, or zero, which is a real number that is neither positive nor negative.
- For each positive real number, *a*, there exists a negative real number, *b*, for which the sum of *a* and *b* is zero. ($a + b = 0$)
- The sum of any real number, *a*, and zero, is *a*. So, $a + 0 = a$.
- The order in which two real numbers are added does not change the sum. So, $a + b = b + a$. This is referred to as the commutative property.
- The order in which three or more real numbers are added does not change the sum. So, $(a + b) + c = a + (b + c)$. This is referred to as the associative property.

Phew! That was a lot of information just about addition! We won't cover every operation in as much detail. After all, you do have a test to take at some point! However, this detail has allowed us to discuss some useful ways to think and learn about math. You'll detect many of these same quantitative reasoning strategies in subsequent discussions and in solutions to problems.

Moreover, never underestimate the ability of the GMAT or GRE test-writers to construct problems about basic concepts such as the addition of integers.

Consider this problem:

> For which of the following pairs of integers, *a* and *b*, is $a + b > a$ and $a + b < b$?
>
> (A) $a = 5, b = 2$
> (B) $a = 5, b = 0$
> (C) $a = 0, b = 2$
> (D) $a = -5, b = 2$
> (E) $a = -5, b = -2$

Let's look at two different solutions for this problem. As discussed earlier, it's always good to think about different ways to solve problems.

Solution 1: One of the easiest ways to solve this problem is to simply plug the numbers into the inequalities until you find the one that works. For (A), $5 + 2 > 5$ is a true statement but $5 + 2 < 2$ is false, so eliminate (A). For (B), $5 + 0 > 5$ is false and $5 + 0 < 0$ is also false, so eliminate (B). For (C), $0 + 2 > 2$ is false and $0 + 2 < 2$ is also false, so eliminate (C). For (D), $-5 + 2 > -5$ is true and $-5 + 2 < 2$ is true, so keep (D). For (E), $-5 + (-2) > -5$ is false and $-5 + (-2) < -2$ is true, so eliminate (E). The correct answer is (D).

Solution 2: Based on the rules that we studied, if both numbers are positive, then the sum is greater than both numbers. So, eliminate (A). If both numbers are negative, then the sum is less than both numbers. So, eliminate (E). If one of the numbers is zero, then the sum is equal to the other number. So, eliminate (B) and (C). Based on the rules, it's also possible to realize that the only way that the sum can be greater than one number and less than the other is for one number to be positive and the other to be negative. Only (D) includes one positive number and one negative number. The correct answer is (D).

Can you think of any other ways to solve this problem?[14]

Subtraction

Subtraction is the inverse operation of addition. We use addition to augment (or add to!) a collection of items and subtraction to take away from that collection. Because the two operations are so connected, you'd think the rules for addition and subtraction would be very similar. But, it ain't so!

Much of the difference[15] between addition and subtraction has to do with the fact that subtraction is not commutative. So, unlike with addition, where $a + b = b + a$, with subtraction $a - b \neq b - a$. There's one exception. Can you think of what it is?[16]

The fact that subtraction is not commutative, which is referred to as **anticommutative,**[17] means that most of the rules that we defined for addition either don't apply to subtraction or would need to be stated in

---

[14] How about an algebraic solution? Subtract a from both sides of the first inequality to find that $b > 0$. Subtract b from both sides of the second inequality to find that $a < 0$. Only (D) satisfies both those conditions.

[15] I couldn't help myself! I had to use a word that would add to the conversation.

[16] If $a = b$, the $a - b = b - a = 0$

[17] Yet another fun math term that isn't used by the test-writers. We introduce it here only for context.

a much more complicated way. For example, our first rule for addition with integers stated that the sum of two positive integers is also a positive integer. That rule doesn't apply to subtraction because the result of subtracting two positive integers can be a positive integer (5 − 2 = 3), a negative integer (2 − 5 = −3), or zero (2 − 2 = 0). The same holds true for subtracting two negative numbers. The result can be positive (−2 − (−5) = 3), negative (−5 − (−2) = −3), or zero (−3 − (−3) = 0).[18]

We're going to pause for a moment to review an important aspect of the algorithm for subtraction. When subtracting by a negative number, as we did in those last examples, the effect is to add the second number to the first number. That's true whether the first number is positive, negative, or zero. For example, −2 − (−5) = −2 + 5 = 3. In the same way, 2 − (−5) = 2 + 5 = 7. As a final example, 0 − (−5) = 0 + 5 = 5. In each example, the first instance, a subtraction problem, is equivalent to the second instance, an addition problem.

Why is it the case that subtracting by a negative number is equivalent to adding by a positive number? Let's go back to our prehistoric ancestors for a moment. They would have developed subtraction out of the concept of removing something or taking something away. If you have 5 berries and eat 2 of the berries, you have 3 berries left. Eventually, that problem turns into our more modern (and abstract) version 5 − 3 = 2, where we just work with numbers and leave the berries behind. We also discussed how working subtraction problems with numbers eventually led to the integers because subtraction with the natural numbers is only possible when the first number is greater than or equal to the second in the subtraction problem.

So, when we say 3 − 3 = 0, that makes sense from the standpoint of subtraction being an operation that takes something away. We started out with 3, took 3 away, and we were left with nothing. That makes sense for berries and for numbers! But, what if we started with −3 and wanted to wind up with nothing? What would we need to take away? Following the model that we described for positive numbers, we'd need to take away (or subtract) everything that we started with. So, if we

---

[18] As a result, we'd need to state rules in terms of cases. For example, the difference of two positive numbers, a and b, is a positive number c, if $a > b$. Furthermore, the difference of two positive numbers, a and b, is a negative number, c, if $a < b$.

started with −3, we'd need to subtract −3 to wind up with 0. Therefore, −3 − (−3) must be equivalent to −3 + 3 = 0. By extension, subtracting by a negative number is equivalent to adding by the positive of that number (aka the additive inverse).

Now that we've reviewed subtracting with a negative number, let's get back to the consequences of subtraction not being commutative. Because subtraction is not commutative, it's also not associative. In other words, $(a − b) − c \neq a − (b − c)$. For example, $(7 − 3) − 2 \neq 7 − (3 − 2)$. So, the order in which a string of numbers is subtracted affects the result. The fact that subtraction is not associative means that it's necessary to determine an order of operations. Here, the numbers enclosed in parentheses are subtracted first. If there are no parentheses, subtract from left to right. If that's starting to sound familiar, you are probably thinking of PEMDAS, the order of operations for calculations that involve more than one basic operation. We'll review PEMDAS once we've introduced the other basic operations.

Zero can still play the role of an identity element for subtraction, but only if we are careful to specify the order in which we subtract. See! There's that lack of commutativity for subtraction rearing its head again!

To summarize the rules for subtraction:

- The difference of two real numbers can be a positive real number, a negative real number, or zero, which is a real number that is neither positive nor negative.
- The difference of any real number and zero is that real number. So, $a − 0 = a$, where a is any real number. However, $0 − a = −a$.
- Subtraction is not commutative. So, $a − b \neq b − a$ unless $a = b$. Subtraction is anticommutative.
- Subtraction is not associative. So, $(a − b) − c \neq a − (b − c)$.

Multiplication

Multiplication may have evolved as a shorthand for repeated addition.[19] You were probably first introduced to multiplication in this way. For example, 2×5 can be interpreted as adding 5 two times. So, $2 \times 5 = 5 + 5$. Because multiplication starts as a shorthand for repeated

---

[19] The ancient Egyptians performed multiplication as a series of successive sums.

addition, it shouldn't be too surprising that many of the properties of addition are also properties of multiplication.

Here are some of the important rules that apply to multiplication with real numbers.

- There are 3 basic rules that describe whether the **product** of two real numbers is a positive or a negative real number.
  - Positive × Positive = Positive
  - Positive × Negative = Negative
    (Also, Negative × Positive = Negative)
  - Negative × Negative = Positive
- Multiplication over addition or subtraction uses the **distributive property**.
  - $a \times (b + c) = (a \times b) + (a \times c)$
  - $a \times (b - c) = (a \times b) - (a \times c)$
- The product of any real number and zero is zero. So, $a \times 0 = 0$, where a is any real number.
- The product of any real number and one is that real number. So, $a \times 1 = a$, where a is any real number.
- Multiplying a real number by −1 yields the additive inverse of that number. So, $a \times (-1) = -a$, where a is a real number.
- The order in which two real numbers are multiplied does not change the product. So, $a \times b = b \times a$. This is referred to as the commutative property.
- The order in which three or more real numbers are multiplied does not change the product. So, $(a \times b) \times c = a \times (b \times c)$. This is referred to as the associative property.

- For all real numbers x, such that $x \neq 0$, there exists a real number $\frac{1}{x}$, such that $x\left(\frac{1}{x}\right) = 1$. The number $\frac{1}{x}$ is called the **multiplicative inverse** or the **reciprocal**.
- Multiplication of two positive real numbers by a positive real number preserves the order of the two original numbers for the products. Multiplication of two positive real numbers by a negative real number reverses the order of the two original numbers for the products.
  - If a, b, and c are positive real numbers and $b > c$, then $ab > ac$.
  - If a is a negative real number and b and c are positive real numbers such that $b > c$, then $ab < ac$.

Let's discuss a few of these rules. We'll start with the first rule.

Multiplication of Positive and Negative Numbers

As we've already discussed, one way to think about multiplication is as a shorthand for repeated addition. Earlier, we illustrated that idea with an example using two positive numbers. It's easy enough to extend that model to the multiplication of one positive number and one negative number. For example, we can think of $2 \times (-5)$ as adding $-5 + (-5)$ to get a sum of -10. So, it certainly makes sense that the product of a positive and a negative number is a negative number.

However, when we get to the product of two negative numbers, the model breaks down. How should one interpret a problem such as $(-2) \times (-5)$? Are we adding -5 to itself -2 times? That just doesn't make any sense, does it? Yet, we have that rule that we've all known since primary school that negative $\times$ negative = positive. What's up with this rule?

First off, we're going to abandon the model. In the study of math, it's sometimes necessary to abandon the model. As mathematical topics become more general, they sometimes leave behind the model that was the original inspiration behind the concept. We've already seen an example of that when we discussed numbers. Natural numbers exist to count things. However, as math progressed, we simply found that we needed other types of numbers, such as integers or fractions, to solve problems, even though those numbers cannot be used to count things in the same way that natural numbers can.

Next, we need to again invoke the spectre of the Dead Mathematicians and their Dead Mathematician Rules! We last encountered this group when we discussed why zero is a natural number. At that time, we stated that sometimes mathematicians go with the convention that produces the most useful results. That's the story with this rule.

To understand why it's convenient to define the product of two negative numbers as a positive number, we need to take a look at two of our other rules. When we discussed addition, we introduced additive inverses. As a quick review, additive inverses are two numbers, such as

3 and −3, that have a sum of zero. It's helpful to have a way to find the additive inverse of a number. If we want to find the additive inverse of a positive number, we can multiply that number by −1 to get the corresponding negative number. In other words, we can agree that $(-1) \times 3 = -3$. But, what if we start with −3 and want to find its additive inverse? Shouldn't we be able to do the same thing? In that case, $(-1) \times (-3) = 3$. In other words, the rule about the product of two negative numbers helps to define the useful concept of additive inverses.

Distributive Property

Next up, there's the distributive property. The distributive property is a big deal on both the GMAT and the GRE.[20] The property's primary use is in factoring algebraic expressions. For now, however, let's make sure that we understand how the distributive property works with numbers.

As we've done before, we'll start with some examples. Let's imagine what the discovery of the distributive property might have looked like for some early mathematicians. One day a group of mathematicians are doing what mathematicians do—they are playing around with some numbers. One of them notices something interesting: $2 \times 5 - (2 \times 3) + (2 \times 2)$. In other words, one of the numbers in the multiplication problem, in this case 5, can be rewritten as the sum of two other numbers. When each of the numbers in the sum is multiplied by the other number in the multiplication problem, in this case 2, and the sum of the two products is taken, the result is the same as that of the original multiplication problem. Intrigued, our mathematician tries out some other numbers. Soon, the whole group of mathematicians is trying out other numbers and they keep finding that the result works for all the numbers that they try.

A few members of the group start to wonder whether they can also rewrite one of the numbers as the difference of two other numbers. For example, what if 5 is written as $7 - 2$? Does $2 \times 5 = (2 \times 7) - (2 \times 2)$? It does! Our group of mathematicians tests the result with other numbers. After some additional work, they are ready to state two versions of the distributive property. One works for multiplication over addition: $a \times (b + c) = (a \times b) + (a \times c)$. The other works for multiplication over subtraction: $a \times (b - c) = (a \times b) - (a \times c)$.

---

[20] And in math, in general!

It turns out that the distributive property is very useful. For one thing, the distributive property can be used to simplify the calculations required when multiplying. For example, suppose we need to solve 12×14. We could use the distributive property to rewrite the problem as $12 \times 14 = 12 \times (7 + 7) = (12 \times 7) + (12 \times 7) = 84 + 84 = 168$.[21] That may not seem so revolutionary, but keep in mind that for most of history, math was done without the benefit of calculators or computers.[22]

By the time that negative numbers came into use, the distributive property was entrenched. It was so useful that nobody wanted to give it up and that forced the definition for finding the product of two negative numbers. Suppose that we want to find the product of $(-2) \times (-5)$. We'd start with math properties that we already know and use. We might start with the rule that the product of any number and zero is zero. Now we can use the additive inverse idea to write 0 in a special way. Our goal is to get a problem written in a way that allows us to use the distributive property. So, we write a different problem: $(-2) \times (5 + -5) = 0$. Because 5 and -5 are additive inverses, their sum is 0. Now, however, we can use the distributive rule: $(-2) \times (5 + -5) = (-2 \times 5) + (-2 \times -5) = 0$. Because $(-2) \times 5 = -10$, the problem can now be written as $-10 + (-2 \times -5) = 0$. So, now we face a choice. We can either say that $(-2) \times (-5) = 10$ (and hence that the product of two negative numbers is a positive number) or we can abandon useful concepts such as additive inverses, multiplying by 0 yields 0, and the distributive property. The Dead Mathematicians have made their choice: the product of two negative numbers is a positive number!

Multiplying by Zero, One, and Negative One

Let's go back to one of the properties that we just used: multiplying by 0 yields 0. This property is one of three properties that we defined above which give rules for multiplication by the special numbers 0, 1, and -1. The property that multiplying by 0 yields 0 is often an important property for interpreting statements that put constraints on the numbers used in GMAT and GRE math problems. For example, if a problem states that $ab \neq 0$, it means that neither a nor b equals zero. If a problem states that $ab = 0$, it means that a or b or both equal zero.

---

[21] Some ancient cultures did, in fact, solve multiplication problems as a series of sums.

[22] As a reminder, the math section of the GMAT is also done without the benefit of a calculator. So, it's a good idea to brush up on ways to calculate with numbers. Using the distributive property is one way to simplify some calculations.

For addition, we stated that 0 is the identity element because $a + 0 = a$, for all real a. Zero is not the identity element for multiplication, however, because $a \times 0 = a$ is true only when $a = 0$. Instead, 1 plays the role of identity element for multiplication because $a \times 1 = a$ for all real a. Many GMAT and GRE problems ask you to decide whether a mathematical statement is always true. For these problems, it's often necessary to consider what happens when special numbers such as 1 or 0 are used.

As mentioned above, multiplication by –1 also plays a special role because doing so produces the additive inverse of any real number. This concept, along with the idea of inverse operations, is one of the keys to solving many algebraic equations. Multiplication by –1 can also help us to understand an important rule for working with relational operators.

Multiplication and Inequalities

We've all heard the rule that when multiplying or dividing both sides of an inequality by a negative number, you flip the "sign." In this case, the "sign" refers to the inequality symbol, which is also known as one of the relational operators: >, ≥, <, or ≤. Why do we substitute one relational operator for another in this situation?

Consider two numbers such as 3 and 4. We can say that $3 < 4$. Now, let's form the additive inverses of these two numbers by multiplying each number by –1: $-1 \times 3 = -3$ and $-1 \times 4 = -4$. If we don't want to change the order of the numbers in the inequality, we need to switch the less than relational operator to the greater than relational operator so that we can state $-3 > -4$. This need to change the relational operator extends to multiplying or dividing by other negative numbers.

This discussion brings us to the last rule that we stated for multiplication. In effect, multiplying two numbers by a positive number preserves the order of those two numbers in the product. However, multiplying two numbers by a negative number reverses the order of those two numbers in the product. When solving GMAT or GRE problems that require evaluating whether a mathematical statement is always true, it is often helpful to remember that multiplying by a negative number can reverse the order of terms.[23]

---

[23] On the GRE, Quantitative Comparison problems sometimes require this type of analysis. On the GMAT, Data Sufficiency questions sometimes play this role.

Multiplicative Inverses

We'll quickly mention one other property before moving on to division. All non-zero real numbers have a multiplicative inverse. The product of a number and its multiplicative inverse is one. To find the multiplicative inverse of a number, divide 1 by the number. For example, the multiplicative inverse of 2 is $\frac{1}{2}$ because $2 \times \frac{1}{2} = 1$. You may be thinking that the multiplicative inverse sounds a lot like a reciprocal. That's because multiplicative inverse is just another term for reciprocal! However, most people think of a reciprocal as "flipping a number upside down." That's an okay definition for most problems, but there are GMAT and GRE problems for which it's important to know that two numbers, *m* and *n*, are reciprocals (or multiplicative inverses!) if *mn* = 1.

Division

Now it's time to discuss division, which, in most circumstances, is the inverse operation of multiplication. We need to say *in most circumstances* for two reasons. First, while the product of two integers is an integer, the **quotient**[24] of two integers is not always an integer. Second, while the product of 0 and any real number is 0, division by 0 is undefined. So, in most cases, division is the inverse operation of multiplication, however, that classification comes with some caveats.

Here are the basic rules that apply to division with real numbers.

- There are 3 basic rules that describe whether the quotient of two real numbers is a positive or a negative real number.
  - Positive ÷ Positive = Positive
  - Positive ÷ Negative = Negative
    (Also, Negative ÷ Positive = Negative)
  - Negative ÷ Negative = Positive

---

[24] The quotient is the result of division. For example, in the division problem 6 ÷ 3 = 2, the quotient is 2.

- For all non-zero real numbers, a, $0 \div a = 0$.
- The quotient of any real number, including 0, and 0 is undefined.
- The quotient of any real number and 1 is that real number. So, $a \div 1 = a$, where a is any real number.
- Division is not commutative. So, $a \div b \neq b \div a$, unless $a = b$.
- Division is not associative. So, $(a \div b) \div c \neq a \div (b \div c)$.

Many of these properties are similar to properties that we have discussed for other operations. However, division is different from the other three operations that we have considered. When any of the operations addition, subtraction, and multiplication are performed with integers, the result is also an integer. In our discussion of subtraction, we discussed how subtraction could be viewed as a motivation for the development of the integers from the natural numbers because the results of some subtraction problems, such as $3 - 7$, cannot be expressed as a natural number. In a similar way, division can be seen as a motivation for the development of rational numbers because the result of dividing two integers, such as $3 \div 2$, is often not an integer.

For division, 1 is the identity element. In other words, dividing any number by 1 produces that number as the quotient. For example, $5 \div 1 = 5$. The same can also be said of numbers that aren't integers. For example, $\frac{1}{2} \div 1 = \frac{1}{2}$. Most people think that division always works the way it does for most natural numbers. In other words, the result of division is a smaller number. Except that it's not! Dividing by 1 doesn't produce a smaller number. Dividing a positive integer by a positive fraction produces a larger number. Test-writers like to take advantage of the bad assumptions that test-takers make. That's why it's important to remember identity elements! Identity elements help us to evaluate whether a mathematical statement is true for all numbers.

Before moving on, let's discuss why division by zero is undefined and how that comes up on the GMAT and GRE. For that, we need to go back to the idea of inverse operations. As discussed earlier, inverse operations basically undo each other. Subtracting 3, for example, undoes adding 3. In most cases, multiplication and division are inverse operations.

Here's a slightly more mathy way to look at the idea that multiplication and division are inverse operations. If we say that $a \times b = c$, then we should be able to get back to a by dividing c by b: $a = c \div b$.[25] Now, look what happens when we make $b = 0$. If $b = 0$, then $c = a \times 0 = 0$. Can we recover the value of a as we did before? We can't, because a could have been any number. In other words, both 1×0 and 2×0 produce a product of 0. So, if we try to undo multiplying by 0 by dividing by 0, should we get 1 or 2 as the result? Obviously, we can then make that claim for any number! In effect, the uniqueness of division breaks down when dividing by 0. So, what have the Dead Mathematicians decreed? They have decreed that dividing by 0 is undefined!

In GMAT and GRE problems, you'll often see conditions or constraints such as $x \neq 0$. In effect, these statements are usually technical requirements of the problem. For example, if a problem wants you to consider the fraction $\dfrac{a}{x}$, the problem will need to state that $x \neq 0$. Otherwise, some test-taker could rightly claim that the credited answer isn't wholly correct because the result would be undefined if $x = 0$. In most cases, statements such as $x \neq 0$ don't change the way that you solve the problem. Those statements are just there to ensure that test-takers can't challenge the problem.

Exponents and Roots

Exponents are used to indicate repeated multiplication. The exponent indicates the number of times to multiply the number, which is referred to as the **base**. For example, 2^3 indicates that the base, 2, should be multiplied 3 times. So, $2^3 = 2 \times 2 \times 2 = 8$.

Exponents are distributive across multiplication. So, $(ab)^c = (a^c)(b^c)$. For example, $(2 \times 3)^2 = (2^2)(3^2)$. Both sides of this equation evaluate to 36. We'll pause for a moment to note that it's important not to forget

---

[25] Hopefully, you still have your pencil in hand and are trying out examples when you read these types of statements to understand them better! Here, for example, you could say $a = 2, b = 4$ and $c = 2 \times 4 = 8$. Does $2 = 8 \div 4$? It does!

to apply the exponent to all the numbers or variables that are being multiplied inside the parentheses. Forgetting to do that is a common mistake that GMAT and GRE test-takers make when solving problems that include exponents.

As long as we're on the topic, here's another common mistake that test-takers make. Exponents do not distribute across addition or subtraction. In other words, $(a + b)^c \neq a^c + b^c$. To see that exponents don't distribute across addition or subtraction, try an example. Does $(2 + 3)^2 = 2^2 + 3^2$? No! The left side of the equation evaluates to 25 but the right side of the equation evaluates to 16. This mistake, trying to distribute an exponent across addition or subtraction, is often made when working with algebraic expressions.

Exponents can be applied to any real number, including fractions, negative numbers, zero, and irrational numbers such as π. Exponents themselves also do not need to be positive integers. Exponents can be negative, fractions, or zero. For these exponents, the model of exponents indicating repeated multiplication of the base must be abandoned.

Exponentiation also needs an inverse operation. Really, it's more proper to speak of exponentiation as having inverse operations. Taking a root is the inverse operation of raising a number to a power. However, the specific root that is required depends on the exponent. So, the relationship here is more nuanced than the relationship between, for example, addition and subtraction as inverse operations.

Let's start with the most familiar type of root—the **square root**. Square roots are used to find the number that, when multiplied by itself, produces the number under the radical. For example, $\sqrt{4}$ means to find the number that, multiplied by itself, equals 4, the number under the radical. In this case, $\sqrt{4} = 2$ because $2 \times 2 = 4$. **Squaring a number** and taking a square root of that number squared undo each other. Hence, squaring a number and taking a square root are inverse operations.

Note that only nonnegative real numbers have square roots that are also real numbers. For example, $\sqrt{-4}$ does not produce a real result because no real number times itself has a product of -4. You may recall from school that the square root of a negative number produces a complex number as its result. While that's true, we don't need to worry about that for the GMAT or GRE. For both tests, all numbers used are real numbers, so neither the GMAT nor the GRE will ask you to find the square root of a negative number. However, in problems that deal with square roots, you may see a statement such as "For all $x \geq 0$, if $\sqrt{x}$ ...." In these problems, the condition that $x \geq 0$ is a technical requirement of the problem. The condition is basically the test-writer's way of reminding you that you only need to consider real numbers when solving problems.

Cube roots are also commonly used on both the GMAT and GRE. **Cube roots** are the inverse operation of cubing a number. Cube roots are used to find the number that, when multiplied by itself three times, produces the number under the radical. For example, $\sqrt[3]{8}$ means to find the number that, multiplied by itself three times, equals 8, the number under the radical. In this case, $\sqrt[3]{8} = 2$ because $2 \times 2 \times 2 = 8$. **Cubing a number**[26] and taking the cube root of a number undo each other. Hence, cubing a number and taking a cube root are inverse operations.

Unlike square roots, cube roots have real results when applied to negative numbers. Because the product of three negative numbers is a negative number, there are real roots for negative numbers. For example, $\sqrt[3]{-8} = -2$ because $(-2) \times (-2) \times (-2) = -8$.

There are also fourth roots, fifth roots, etc., of numbers.[27] However, neither the GMAT nor the GRE generally asks you to work with or compute roots other than square or cube roots.

We have one more topic to discuss before closing this section. Now, that we've introduced the basic operations, we need to discuss what to do when multiple operations are used. Yes, it's time for the order of operations aka PEMDAS!

---

[26] Why do we refer to raising a number to the second power as squaring the number? Why do we refer to raising a number to the third power as cubing the number? Raising a number to the second power yields the area of a square with that number as the length of the sides. Raising a number to the third power yields the volume of a cube with that number as the length of its sides. There was a time when most math was the study of geometry!

[27] That little 3 next to the radical in the cube root symbol represents the power of the root. The two is usually omitted when writing the symbol for a square root. The symbol for a fourth root is $\sqrt[4]{x}$.

Order of Operations

As symbols began to replace words in the study of mathematics,[28] it became necessary to agree upon certain conventions. Prior to the advent of these conventions, math texts often had a few pages at the beginning wherein the author would explain the symbols and conventions used in the text. Imagine needing to learn an entirely new set of symbols and conventions for each math text that you needed (or wanted) to learn!

Of course, it's a little bit of an overstatement to say that the conventions were entirely new from text to text. There were certain conventions that probably carried over from the way that words were used to describe and solve problems. For example, the fact that multiplication distributes over addition and subtraction and that this distributive property is very useful meant that the authors of most texts would set up their symbols to reflect the precedence of multiplication over addition and subtraction. It's somewhat analogous to the way that spelling worked in English prior to the standardization of rules for spelling words. While two different authors might spell a given word differently, those different spellings were still usually tied to the phonetics of the word, and the words were employed according to the grammatical conventions that had evolved.

Okay, enough history. We just wanted to pause long enough to realize that conventions for which operator takes precedence are necessary. Otherwise, it would be possible to get different answers when calculating a problem such as $2 + 3 \times 4$. If addition takes precedence, or if operations are always performed left to right, the answer would be $2 + 3 \times 4 = 5 \times 4 = 20$. However, if multiplication takes precedence, which is our convention, then the answer is $2 + 12 = 14$.

Of course, one way to avoid ambiguity in a statement such as $2 + 3 \times 4$ is to use parentheses. In fact, even with the convention to evaluate multiplication before addition in place, $2 + 3 \times 4$ is often written as

---

[28] Prior to the development of algebra, problems and solutions to those problems were often described using words rather than symbols. Of course, the notion of using symbols to express mathematical ideas is very old. Ancient civilizations had symbols to represent numbers. The ancient Egyptians had symbols to represent the use of a fraction. However, algebra is used to express general solutions to problems. An arithmetic problem might ask "If Jack is 12 years old, how old will he be in 2 years?," while an algebra problem may ask for a more general solution to the idea of adding 2 years to Jack's age: "If Jack is x years old, how old will he be in 2 years?"

$2 + (3 \times 4)$ to distinguish this problem from $(2 + 3) \times 4$. However, the use of parentheses to indicate the order of operations starts to become complicated when considering algebraic expressions. For example, consider an expression such as $2x^2 + 3x$. Because we're all so used to the PEMDAS conventions, we understand the meaning: square the first x, then multiply it by 2, multiply the second x by 3, then add the two products. If we relied on parentheses rather than having conventions for the order of operations, the expression would need to be written $((2(x^2)) + (3x))$. Even there, we'd be following the convention that nested parentheses are evaluated from the inside to the outside.

To avoid the need to use so many parentheses, the conventions we know as PEMDAS developed.[29] PEMDAS, of course, is the acronym used in the United States to remember the order of operations.[30] The letters in the acronym represent Parentheses, Exponents, Multiplication and Division, and Addition and Subtraction. Expressions inside parentheses have a higher order of precedence than anything else, so evaluate those expressions first. If there are nested parentheses, evaluate from the inside to the outside. Then, evaluate any exponents. If an expression contains both multiplication and division, evaluate from left to right. For example, $12 \times 10 \div 3 = 40$. If an expression contains both addition and subtraction, also evaluate from left to right.

While you do need to know the order of operations, neither the GMAT nor the GRE explicitly tests the order of operations. So, you won't be asked to evaluate a complicated expression such as $14 + 8 \div 2 - 10$.[31] However, as discussed, standard ways of writing algebraic expressions and equations, such as $2x^2 + 3x - 4 = 0$, make implicit use of the order of operations. You'll also use the order of operations for certain geometry and other formulas. In many cases, your use of the order of operations has become so ingrained that you don't even realize that you are using the order of operations! However, when in doubt about which operation to perform first, be guided by PEMDAS!

---

[29] The acronym PEMDAS itself and strict drilling of its use in complicated expressions is a relatively modern invention. While the history is somewhat murky, it seems to have developed in the late 1800s and is tied to the development of the textbook market for public schools. It's not known who came up with the acronym or who Aunt Sally was. The order of operations as a set of conventions used by mathematicians predates the usage of the acronym.

[30] Other countries have different acronyms such as BEDMAS, where the B refers to brackets. Or, BOD-MAS, where the B refers to brackets and the O refers to orders.

[31] The answer is 8. First, do the division to get $14 + 4 - 10$. Then evaluate left to right.

Here's a slightly different way to write and remember most parts of the order of operations.

E

M D

A S

Here, the idea is to focus on the hierarchical structure of the order of operations. Exponentiation takes precedence over the four operations below it in the diagram. Similarly, multiplication and division take precedence over addition and subtraction. Multiplication is listed to the left of division, and addition is listed to the left of subtraction. So, the left to right order in which these operations are evaluated is reflected in the diagram.

This diagram also shows how operations are distributed over other operations. Each operation distributes over the operations immediately below it in the diagram. So, as discussed, exponents distribute over multiplication and division.[32] Multiplication and division distribute over addition and subtraction.

This diagram doesn't include parentheses because parentheses are not an operation. Because parentheses are not an operation, they don't distribute over anything. So, it would be hard to place parentheses on the diagram without losing other information conveyed by the diagram. Nonetheless, this diagram can be quite useful as long as you remember to evaluate anything in parentheses first!

---

[32] Note, however, that we said *immediately below*. Remember that exponents don't distribute over addition and subtraction.

Let's Give It a Try

The writers of the GMAT and GRE can test the rules of operations in various ways.

Here's one example:

> If the symbol Ψ represents one of the operations addition, subtraction, and multiplication, and $a \Psi (b \Psi c) = a \Psi (c \Psi b)$ for some a, b, and c, which of the following could be the operation represented by Ψ?
>
> (A) Addition only
> (B) Subtraction only
> (C) Multiplication only
> (D) Addition and Subtraction only
> (E) Addition and Multiplication only

We'll continue to build out the skill of thinking about multiple ways to solve problems by looking at two solutions for this problem.

Before we do that, however, a quick word of advice. Don't be thrown by the Greek letter in the problem! The symbol is certainly designed to make you say "But wait! No math teacher that I've ever had told me what that means!" However, when GMAT or GRE problems use an unfamiliar symbol, the meaning of that symbol is defined in the problem. In this problem, for example, the problem states that the symbol represents one of the three operations: addition, subtraction, or multiplication. So, each time the symbol is used in the problem, it is replaced by one of the operations. However, each time the symbol is used, it must be replaced with the same operation. So, in evaluating the equation, if the first symbol represents addition, the other three symbols also represent addition.

Solution 1: Use numbers to evaluate the equation for each of the three possible operations. For example, let $a = 10$, $b = 4$, and $c = 2$. First evaluate the equation using addition in place of the symbol. Does $10 + (4 + 2) = 10 + (2 + 4)$? It does, so addition is part of the correct answer. Next, evaluate the equation with subtraction in place of the symbol. Does $10 - (4 - 2) = 10 - (2 - 4)$? In this case, the left side of the equation evaluates to 8 but the right side evaluates to 12.[33] So, subtraction is not part of the correct answer. Finally, evaluate the equation using multiplication in place of the symbol. Does $10 \times (4 \times 2) = 10 \times (2 \times 4)$? It does, so multiplication is also part of the correct answer. The correct answer is (E), addition and multiplication only.

Solution 2: It's also possible to take a rules-based approach to solving this problem. For the left side of the equation to be equal to the right side, $b \, \Psi \, c$ must equal $c \, \Psi \, b$. That means the operation represented by Ψ must be commutative. Of the possible operations that Ψ could represent, only addition and multiplication are commutative. Hence, the answer must be (E), addition and multiplication only.

A Quick Thought about this Section

Good job! You've successfully completed this long but important section!

This section introduced a lot of the quantitative reasoning skills that we'll discuss in the next section. It also may help you to understand some of the language (and the reasons for that language) used in math problems on the GMAT and GRE. It may have even helped you to think about math a little differently!

---

[33] Remember that the expression inside the parentheses is evaluated first.

PART III

Quantitative Reasoning

In the next two chapters, we're going to look at some of the quantitative reasoning skills that get tested in GMAT and GRE problems. Our approach will be problem-based and we'll review concepts as needed. In this fashion, you will see how these skills can help you to solve problems.

Not every GMAT nor GRE problem needs one or more of these skills for its solution. Some GMAT and GRE problems are simply designed to test whether you know a particular rule or can perform a certain operation. However, some harder questions are harder precisely because they don't rely on an easily recognizable rule or operation. For some problems, it can even be hard to detect which concepts—such as averages or prime factors—are being tested. Such problems may leave you feeling as though you've hit a brick wall. Alternatively, these problems can leave you confused about how to get started because there are seemingly too many paths forward.

Such problems may leave you feeling as though an unfamiliar concept is being tested. You may also feel as though the problem lacks essential details. From the test-writers' perspective, these are the problems that most clearly test quantitative reasoning skills. Remember that testing quantitative reasoning is a major design goal of both the GMAT and GRE. Some of these problems ask about advanced mathematical concepts in ways that don't actually reference those advanced concepts by name or notation. One of the first problems that we discussed in this book worked that way. The solution depended on the Pigeonhole Principle, but we were able to solve the problem without reference to the principle by name. In other words, you may be able to solve questions that test quantitative reasoning skills even if you've never studied the advanced concept embedded in the question. For the test-writers, that's an indication of quantitative reasoning ability!

It's also true that the lines blur between some of these skills. There's overlap. Some problems test more than one quantitative reasoning skill. Some problems in this section could have been placed in different categories. So, the skills aren't exactly a checklist that you can run through when you encounter a difficult problem. Rather, these skills are skills to practice as you prepare for your test. Pay attention to the problems for which you aren't immediately sure how to proceed. As you start to notice some of the quantitative reasoning skills necessary to solve such problems, you'll become more adept at using these skills.

Let's get started!

CHAPTER 5

What to
Look For

Look for Order

Our first topic concerns order. Mathematicians love order. Actually, human beings are more or less hard-wired to look for order. Even if you consider yourself a messy person, you still deal with order on a daily basis. We adhere to schedules (or at least try to!), use money that can be ordered by value, and generally try to avoid as much chaos as we can!

In some ways, mathematics is the study of order. Mathematicians look for order and structure in the objects that they study. One of our first mathematical activities—as both individuals and as a species—involves learning to count, an exercise in learning about order.

As a result, it's probably not surprising that some problems in a section designed to test quantitative reasoning involve looking for order. Let's look at a few examples.

Begin at the Beginning

Fermat primes are prime numbers that can be written in the form $2^{2^n} + 1$ where n is an integer. Which of the following is a Fermat prime?

(A) 1
(B) 2
(C) 7
(D) 17
(E) 31

Solution: One of the things that mathematicians love to do is to look for order. Sometimes that means looking for numbers that share a certain property. Properties of even or odd and positive or negative are well-known examples of looking for numbers that share a certain property. Mathematicians have cataloged many different ways to classify prime numbers that share certain properties. Fermat primes are one such way of classifying prime numbers. This question tests your ability to look for a certain type of order that exists for some prime numbers.[1]

---

[1] Very few prime numbers seem to actually share this property. There are only five known Fermat primes. Could there be more? Mathematicians are still looking!

One of the things that the writers of the GMAT and GRE love to do is to try to frighten test-takers into thinking that they need to know some bit of esoterica to answer a question. This question takes that strategy. The use of the term *Fermat prime* might cause you to say "But, I've never heard of those! How am I supposed to answer a question about something I've never heard of?" The formula used in the problem also looks intimidating. An exponent that also has an exponent? What's up with that?

So, the first order of business is not to panic! While questions that refer to esoteric terms or that use strange looking formulas may seem intimidating, everything you need to know is in the question. In other words, you don't need prior knowledge of Fermat primes to solve this problem.

Next, we need to settle on a solution strategy. There are two basic strategies that we could employ to solve this problem. We could set each of the numbers in the answer choices equal to the formula and try to solve for n to see whether we get an integer. However, solving for n may not be easy. After all, we'd be solving for a variable that is an exponent and that generally involves math that is beyond the scope of the GMAT or GRE. The second strategy that we could employ is to do our own search for Fermat primes by substituting different values of n into the formula. Because the numbers in the answers are reasonably small, we can just start with a small value for n and try successively larger values until we find a number in the answer choices. This approach is better, so let's get to work!

So, where do we start? The problem states that n is an integer. Of course, there are a lot of integers and we don't want to make assumptions. The answer choices (and prime numbers) are integers. However, negative exponents are ways of writing reciprocals.[2] In other words, if we tried a negative number for n, we wouldn't get an integer as a result. We might be tempted to start at $n = 1$, but there's no reason to exclude 0. So, let's start with $n = 0$.

We need to find the value of $2^{2^0} + 1$. To evaluate, we need to invoke what we can consider a corollary to the PEMDAS rules. PEMDAS tells us that we should evaluate expressions inside parentheses first. The intent of this rule is that we evaluate from the inside to the outside for nested parentheses. Here, we have nested exponents, so we need to do something similar and work from the topmost exponent to the bottom.

---

[2]   For more on negative exponents, check out the bonus chapter in your online Student Tools.

Put another way, the exponent for the 2 at the bottom of our little tower of exponents is 2^0, so we need to evaluate that first.

$$2^{2^0} + 1 = 2^1 + 1 = 3$$

Note that we made use of the zero exponent rule here.[3] The first Fermat prime is 3. That means that we can eliminate (A) and (B) since larger values of n will produce larger values from the formula. We could have also eliminated (A) because 1 is not prime!

We want to make our search methodical so that we don't miss any potential answers. So, quell the impulse to jump to picking a number such as 2 or 3 for n. We're better off just trying $n = 1$ next. Directed, methodical searches are an important tool in mathematics and can be a good strategy to employ when solving test questions.

If $n = 1$, then $2^{2^1} + 1 = 2^2 + 1 = 5$. That's not an answer choice, so we'll keep going.

If $n = 2$, then $2^{2^2} + 1 = 2^4 + 1 = 17$. Hey! That's (D)! We've found the Fermat prime that we were looking for, so we can stop searching. The correct answer is (D).

Using Order to Do Less Work

V is the set of positive odd integers less than 100, and W is the set of the cubes of the numbers in V. How many of the elements that are in Set V are also in Set W?

(A) None
(B) One
(C) Two
(D) Three
(E) Four

---

[3]   As a reminder, for all $x \neq 0$, $x^0 = 1$.

Solution: Here's another question about numbers that share some property. Again, there's some math vocabulary in the question that may seem off-putting. This problem uses the terms *set*, *element*, and *cube*. The actual definition of the term **set** is that a set is a collection of different objects. So, a set could consist of numbers such as 1, 2, and 3 or it could consist of a black pen, a blue pen, and a red pen. A set cannot, however, repeat items. So, 1, 2, and 3 is a set, but 1, 1, 2, and 3 is not a set.[4] The technical definition of set isn't necessary to solve this problem. It's pretty clear from the wording of the problem that we are just supposed to look at all the odd integers less than 100 and all the cubes that are also less than 100.

We also don't need to get too hung up on the meaning of the word *element*. An **element** is just a member of a set. So, in the set 1, 2, 3, it is proper to say that there are three elements. It's also proper to say that 1 is a member of this set. Again, we can probably deduce that the question wants us to look at the numbers that are in both sets, even if the problem-writer chose to refer to those numbers using the math term *elements*.

Finally, there's the term *cubes*. A cube, sometimes also referred to as a *perfect cube*, is an integer that can be obtained by raising some other integer to the third power. For example, 8 is a cube (or perfect cube) because $2^3 = 8$. A cube can also be defined as an integer that has an integer cube root. With this example, 8 is a cube because $\sqrt[3]{8} = 2$. It would be difficult to answer this problem without knowing the definition of cube when referring to numbers.

Now we need a solution strategy. We could write out both sets of numbers, but notice that Set *W*, the set of cubes, is formed from Set *V*, the set of odd integers that are less than 100. So, this question is really just asking how many of the cubes less than 100 are odd integers. We really only need to list out the cubes.

We can also take a shortcut. We don't need to list out all the cubes because we are only interested in the ones that are odd. Because a cube is formed by multiplying a number by itself three times, the

---

[4] 1, 1, 2, and 3 is properly referred to as a **list**. Sets consist of unique objects because Georg Cantor, who developed set theory, said so. The dead mathematicians have spoken!

number that is raised to the third power must be odd to result in an odd cube. That's because the product of two even numbers is even and the product of two odd numbers is odd. It's not a problem to list out all the cubes, even and odd, that are less than 100. If you did that, you'd just need to remember to cross off the cubes that are even.

We'll take the shortcut. The cubes that we are interested in are $1^3 = 1$ and $3^3 = 27$. There are only two elements in Set W, and hence, there are only two numbers in both sets. The correct answer is (C).

Look for Patterns

Closely related to the idea of looking for order is looking for patterns. The solutions to GMAT and GRE problems that involve impossible calculations often involve a pattern. We should stop for a minute to define an impossible calculation in the context of a GMAT or GRE problem. These calculations aren't literally impossible. The calculations can be performed. They just can't be performed in a reasonable amount of time. For example, a problem that asks about the 50th term in a sequence is almost certainly testing whether you can find a pattern.

Mathematics makes use of two distinct styles of formal reasoning—inductive and deductive reasoning. We'll discuss deductive reasoning in a later section.

Inductive reasoning is deeply connected to the idea of looking for patterns. Inductive reasoning involves reasoning from the specific to the general. That often means finding a pattern and making a conclusion about something that is always true based on that pattern. Mathematicians use a more rigorous form of inductive reasoning that allows them to prove conclusions. However, proofs based on inductive reasoning often develop from noticing a pattern.

Neither the GMAT nor the GRE does anything quite that involved with patterns. However, because finding a pattern is often the first step in inductive reasoning, both tests include finding patterns as a way of measuring quantitative reasoning.

Patterns in Digits

What is the 35th digit to the right of the decimal point in the decimal form of $\frac{7}{11}$?

(A) 3
(B) 4
(C) 5
(D) 6
(E) 7

Solutions: Calculate a decimal to 35 places? The test-writers must be mad![5]

Impossible calculations are often an indication that the solution to a problem involves finding a pattern. In this case, we are defining an "impossible calculation" as one that most test-takers could not perform in the 2 to 3 minutes that most high-scoring test-takers need to solve most problems on either the GMAT or GRE. Here, most test-takers, including high-scoring test-takers, could not calculate 35 decimal places in 2 to 3 minutes. So, there must be a pattern.

The way that you find a pattern is that you start writing out the numbers, terms, or digits until you start to see repetitions. In this case, we need to start performing the long division necessary to convert the fraction to a decimal. Here's what the long division looks like after the first digit of the decimal has been found:

$$
\begin{array}{r}
0.6 \\
11\overline{)7.0} \\
\underline{6\,6} \\
4
\end{array}
$$

---

[5] There's a quick caveat for this problem. Most of the problems in this book could be included on either the GMAT or GRE. This problem is an exception in that it would be highly unlikely to be on the GRE because the GRE has an onscreen calculator that would make it very easy to find the pattern. However, the GRE does ask questions for which the solution involves finding a pattern.

One digit isn't sufficient to find a pattern so we'll keep going. Here's what the long division looks like after a few more digits have been calculated.

$$
\begin{array}{r}
0.6363 \\
11\overline{)7.0000} \\
\underline{6\ 6} \\
40 \\
\underline{33} \\
70 \\
\underline{66} \\
40
\end{array}
$$

With four digits calculated, we can see the pattern: $\dfrac{7}{11} = 0.\overline{6363}$. In the decimal expansion of the fraction, the odd digits are 6s and the even digits are 3s. The problem asks for the 35th digit. Because 35 is an odd number, we know that the 35th decimal place in the decimal expansion of the fraction is a 6. The correct answer is (D).

Patterns in Computation

$$
\begin{array}{r}
111 \\
112 \\
113 \\
121 \\
..... \\
+333 \\
\end{array}
$$

The addition problem shown above shows five of the 27 different three-digit integers that can be formed by using only the digits 1, 2, and 3. What is the sum of these 27 integers?

(A) 1,998
(B) 2,700
(C) 3,996
(D) 5,994
(E) 6,660

Solution: Add up 27 integers? And all 27 of those integers aren't even listed in the problem? Yikes!

Again, the impossible nature of the calculation is a good indication that the key to the solving the problem in a reasonable amount of time is to find a pattern and use it! The way to find a pattern is to write out more terms until the pattern becomes clear. The test-writers may have listed only five of the integers so fewer test-takers would realize that there is a pattern.

So, let's go find that pattern!

We won't need to list out the remaining 22 integers to find the pattern. In fact, we only need the next two numbers that come after 121. Those numbers are 122 and 123. So, the first three numbers (111, 112, and 113) and the next three numbers (121, 122, and 123) have a repeating pattern for the **units digits**. This 1, 2, 3 pattern will keep repeating, so we need to determine how many times the pattern repeats for all 27 integers. There are three numbers in each group, so we can just divide the total number of integers by the number of integers in each group to find that there are 27 ÷ 3 = 9 groups.

At this point, we can find the sum of the units digits. The sum of the units digits for each group is 1 + 2 + 3 = 6. There are nine such groups, so the sum of the units digits for all 27 numbers is 9 × 6 = 54. We can actually pick the correct answer at this point. There's only one answer for which the units digit is 4, so the correct answer must be (D). It's always good practice to keep an eye on the answer choices. Sometimes you only need to do part of the calculation to get the answer.

But, you may be wondering how to find the rest of the sum. Let's go back to that idea of groups of numbers. Let's think about the hundreds digits rather than the units digits. We should have an equal number of integers that have 1 for the hundreds digit as have 2 or 3. So, there are nine numbers that have 1 as the units digit, nine that have 2, and nine that have 3. We can extend that logic to realize that there are nine numbers that have 1 for the tens digit, nine that have 2, and nine that have 3. Finally, there are nine numbers that have 1 as the units digit, nine that have 2, and nine that have 3. We can now add up the numbers by place value.

For the hundreds digits:
$(9 \times 100) + (9 \times 200) + (9 \times 300) = 9 \times (100 + 200 + 300) = 5,400$

For the tens digits:
$(9 \times 10) + (9 \times 20) + (9 \times 30) = 9 \times (10 + 20 + 30) = 540$

For the units digits:
$(9 \times 1) + (9 \times 2) + (9 \times 3) = 9 \times (1 + 2 + 3) = 54$

So, the sum of all 27 numbers is $5,400 + 540 + 54 = 5,994$.

The correct answer is (D).

Patterns in Sequences

$$4, 7, -7, \ldots$$

> In the sequence of numbers shown above, the first term is 4. Each even-numbered term is 3 more than the previous term. Each odd-numbered term, after the first, is -1 times the previous term. What is the sum of the first 22 terms?
>
> (A) -7
> (B)   0
> (C)   4
> (D)   7
> (E)   11

Solution: Ugh! The sum of 22 terms! By now, you know what that means. There's going to be a pattern, so it won't be necessary to add up 22 numbers.

Before we get to work on finding the pattern, however, let's take a moment to clarify some terminology used in this question. A *sequence* is a list of numbers and a rule for generating that list. For example, 2, 5, 8, 11... is a sequence because it's a list of numbers, and each number after the first is found by adding 3 to the previous number.

A *term* is a member of the sequence. Terms are referred to by their ordinal position in the sequence. For example, in the sequence 2, 5, 8, 11..., the first term is 2 and the second term is 5.

The problem describes the numbers shown as a sequence. It then proceeds to provide a rule for generating the sequence. That fits the definition of a sequence. We should expect a rule so that we can write out more numbers in the sequence.

This problem also refers to even- and odd-numbered terms as part of the rule for the sequence. The even-numbered terms are all the terms for which their position in the sequence is denoted by an even number. The odd-numbered terms are all the terms for which their position in the sequence is denoted by an odd number. Now we need to distinguish between the name of the term and the value that the term holds. The problem can help us out with this. It refers to the *first term* and states that its value is 4. In other words, first term is the name of the term and the value held by that term is 4. It's analogous to when we say $x = 2$. The name of the variable is x, and the value that it holds is 2. This also means that the first term is an odd-numbered term because one, its ordinal position, is an odd number, even though the value held by that term is an even number. So, it's the name of the term, which is governed by its position in the sequence, that matters when applying the rule.

With that background, we are ready to start finding the values of some additional terms for this sequence. We know the values of the first three terms. So, we need to find the value of the fourth term. The fourth term is an even-numbered term, so we find its value by adding 3 to the value of the previous term. Hence, the value of the fourth term is $-7 + 3 = -4$.

To find the value of the fifth term, an odd-numbered term, multiply the value of the previous term by -1. Hence, the value of the fifth term is $-4 \times -1 = 4$.

To find the value of the sixth term, an even-numbered term, add 3 to the previous term: $4 + 3 = 7$.

So far, the sequence is 4, 7, –7, –4, 4, 7, ...

We could keep going, but we can see the pattern that is starting to repeat. Starting with the first four terms, we see a repeating pattern of 4, 7, −7, −4. Now, note that the sum of the first four terms is 0. The same is true of next four terms. In fact, there are five groups of four terms that account for the first 20 terms of the sequence. Each group has a sum of 0, so the sum of the first 20 terms in this sequence is 0.

Now we just need to find the values of the 21st and 22nd terms. The 20th term is the last term in a group of four numbers, so the value of the 20th term is −4. The 21st term starts the repeating pattern over, so its value is 4, and the value of the 22nd term is 7. Hence, the sum of the first 22 terms is $4 + 7 = 11$. The correct answer is (E).

Look for Symmetry

Symmetry is deeply embedded in the human psyche. Just look at us! The human form itself involves bilateral symmetry.

In a bit of a broader, more mathematical sense, symmetry involves mirror images about an axis. In mathematics, symmetry can be found in geometric figures which may have more than one axis of symmetry. For example, a square can be divided into mirror images by drawing a line through the midpoints of two of its parallel sides or through two opposite vertices. Symmetry can also be found in the graphs of many functions. For example, a parabola, which is the graph of a quadratic function, has an axis of symmetry that runs through the apex of the parabola.

Symmetry can also be more broadly construed as a property of distributions. For example, data can be arranged in a symmetric fashion about the mean. One of the most commonly used distributions, the normal distribution (aka the bell curve), has this property.

Even the number line displays symmetry. For each positive number, there's a negative number. In fact, you'll sometimes see restrictions such as $p < 0 < q$ in problems. If you ask people to pick numbers for p and q that satisfy this restriction, most of those people will pick numbers such as −2 and 2 because the human brain likes symmetry! In fact, the key to solving problems with such a restriction is often to remind ourselves that the numbers don't need to be picked in such a symmetrical fashion.

Let's see how symmetry can show up in some problems.

Using Symmetry to Find Missing Values

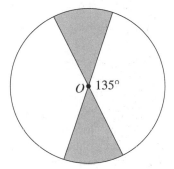

If O is the center of the circle above, what is the ratio of the shaded area of the circular region to that of the unshaded area?

(A)   1:4
(B)   1:3
(C)   2:3
(D)   3:1
(E)   4:1

Solution: There's a lot of symmetry in this figure. If we were to divide the figure in half with a vertical line, the right side is a mirror image of the left side. If we were to divide the figure in half with a horizontal line, the top half of the figure is a mirror image of the bottom half. In fact, any line that connects two points on the circumference of the circle and goes through the center of the circle (aka a diameter!) creates two regions that are mirror images. Mirror images about a line is what symmetry is all about!

Okay, so the figure is symmetrical. How does that help us to solve the problem? The symmetry gives us a way to get started. The figure already shows two lines of symmetry. Let's focus our attention on the one that starts in the upper left and goes to the lower right.

The arrow in the figure below shows this line.

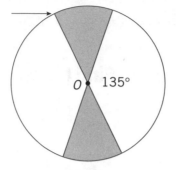

Now, let's focus our attention on the region to the right of this line. The symmetrical nature of the figure means that we can focus on only one half of the figure to get started. Now we can note that there are two adjacent angles on this side of the figure. The degree measure of one of these angles is 135°. To find the degree measure of the other angle, we need only pull out the rule that states that the sum of the degree measures of adjacent angles on a line is 180°. So, the degree measure of the other angle in question is 180° − 135° = 45°.

Now we can use the symmetry of the figure. The region to the left of the line of symmetry also has a larger angle and a smaller angle. Thanks to the symmetry of the figure, those two angles have degree measures that are equal to the degree measures of the corresponding angles in the region to the right of the line of symmetry. The figure below shows the degree measures of the four angles in the figure.

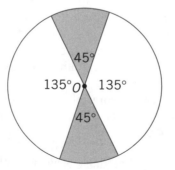

What's that you said? "Didn't we just use the vertical angle rule? Do we really need to use symmetry?" The vertical angle rule, which states that when two lines intersect the opposite angles are equal, is based on symmetry. In effect, each of the two lines that intersect creates an axis of symmetry. So, of course, the opposite angles are equal! Remember that the test-writers are interested in quantitative reasoning. As the test-writers see it, someone who possesses quantitative reasoning ability should be able to deduce the degree measures of the three unmarked angles in the figure even if that person had never heard of vertical angles. How would that person do that? Symmetry!

Now, let's finish the problem. We are asked for the ratio of the shaded area to the unshaded area. Hm, we determined the degree measures of some angles, but we haven't calculated any areas. Is that a problem? No! We can just use the ratio of angles.

Why can we use the ratio of the angles when the problem asks for the ratio of the areas? I'm glad you asked! Asking that question means that you are thinking mathematically. Part of thinking mathematically involves avoiding making assumptions.

To see why we can use the angle measurements, we need to discuss the relationship between a central angle and the arc and sector created by the central angle. Let's review some terminology to clarify our discussion. A *central angle* is the angle between two radii of a circle. In the original figure for this problem, the angle marked 135° is a central angle. The other three angles for which we found the measurements are also central angles.

Central angles let us focus on two parts of the circle. An *arc* is the piece of the circumference of the circle that lies between the two radii that create the central angle. In our original figure for the problem, the arc is the piece of the circumference to the right of the angle marked 135°. To be precise, the arc to the right of the angle marked 135° is a minor arc. The rest of the circumference is referred to as the major arc created by this angle. Problems on the GMAT and GRE generally give arcs names to avoid any confusion.

For example, the minor arc in the figure below is referred to as arc *ABC*.

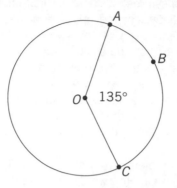

The area between the two radii that create the central angle is called a sector. Essentially, a sector is a pie wedge. In figure above, the sector is the area between radii *AO*, *CO*, and arc *ABC*.

Now that we've brushed up on circle terminology, we can describe the relationship between the central angle and the arc and sector created by that central angle. These relationships are directly proportional. Think about cutting a pizza into four equal slices. To create four equal slices, you'd need to make two cuts, and those cuts would create four 90° angles at the center of the pizza. Each of those slices is a sector of the circle, and the area of each sector is one-fourth the area of the circle. The crust of each slice is one-fourth of the circumference of the pizza.[6] That all makes intuitive sense, right? Now, what's the relationship between the 90° central angles and the area of the sectors and the length of each arc? There are 360° in a circle and $\frac{90}{360} = \frac{1}{4}$. In other words, the ratio of the central angle to the whole circle is the

---

[6] Yes, we are assuming that the pizza is a perfect circle!

same ratio as that of the sector area to the area of the whole circle and to that of the arc to the circumference. Here's that statement written as a formula:

$$\frac{\text{central angle}}{360} = \frac{\text{sector}}{\text{area}} = \frac{\text{arc}}{\text{circumference}}$$

So, for our problem, we don't need to calculate the areas of the two shaded sectors nor the area of the two unshaded sectors because the areas of these sectors to that of the whole circle are the same as that of the central angles to the degrees in the circle. We can just use the angles that we've already determined. Here's the remainder of the calculation:

$$\frac{\text{shaded area}}{\text{unshaded area}} = \frac{45 + 45}{135 + 135} = \frac{90}{270} = \frac{1}{3}$$

The correct answer is (D).

We learned a lot about symmetry, angles, and circles by solving that problem! Let's look at another one.

Using Symmetry to Confirm Intuition

Kyle drives to work at 60 miles per hour and drives home along a different, longer route at 80 miles per hour. If Kyle's total driving time is $1\frac{1}{2}$ hours and his average speed for the total trip is 70 miles per hour, what was the distance that he drove on his way home from work?

(A)   45
(B)   60
(C)   90
(D)   105
(E)   120

Solution: Here's one of those problems that doesn't seem to supply enough information. We don't know the length of the route Kyle takes to work or the length of the route that he takes home. The problem also doesn't provide the time for either leg of the journey. The only time information that we have is the total driving time. What to do? What to do?

You might be tempted to assume that Kyle spends an equal amount of time driving in each direction. For this problem, that assumption would pay off and you'd get the right answer. The urge to assume that the time spent on each leg of the journey is equal is itself evidence of how humans often naturally look for symmetry! However, it's generally a bad practice to make assumptions when solving math problems on standardized tests. That's because one way that test-writers construct wrong answers is to think about common, but incorrect, assumptions that test-takers might make when solving a problem. So, let's discuss why it's true that Kyle spends half the time on each leg of this journey and our instinct to assume symmetry pays off in this problem. That way, we'll no longer be making an assumption and crossing our fingers in the hopes that the assumption is true!

So, why does it turn out to be true that each leg of the journey takes half the total time? We'll need to review a couple of concepts. First, averages[7] are often affected by weights. For example, if club A has 10 members with an average age of 20 and club B has 40 members with an average age of 30, the average age for the members of both clubs is $\dfrac{(10)(20)+(40)(30)}{10+40} = \dfrac{1400}{50} = 28$. The average age for both clubs is closer to the average age of club B, the club with more members. That makes sense. The fact that club B has more members pulls the average age for both clubs toward club B's average age.

The average age is not the average of the two averages. What would it mean if the average age for both clubs were equal to the average of the

---

[7] For more information on averages and other descriptive statistics, check out our bonus chapter in your online Student Tools.

ages for both clubs? In other words, what condition would need to be met for the average age of both clubs to be $\dfrac{20+30}{2}=25$? For that to happen, both clubs would need to have an equal number of members.

For example, if both clubs had 15 members, the average age would be $\dfrac{(15)(20)+(15)(30)}{15+15}=\dfrac{750}{30}=25$. In other words, both clubs contribute equal weight to the calculation of the average age for both clubs.

Or, we could say that there's symmetry of the weights around the midpoint of the two ages.

Next, let's quickly note the relationship between speed, distance, and time. The relationship is given by the formula, Distance = Rate × Time ($d = rt$). For example, if a car travels at 20 miles per hour for 2 hours, the distance covered is $d = (20)(2) = 40$ miles.

Okay, now we're ready to discuss why the time for both legs of the journey in this problem is the same.

Notice that the problem states that the average speed for the entire journey is 70 miles per hour, and that 70 is also the average of 60 and 80. That the average speed for the whole journey is also the average of the two speeds for each leg of the journey implies that there's some symmetry involved. Because we know that the distances are not the same, the only symmetry possible is with the times.

Let's prove that the times are the same. We can set up two equations using the $d = rt$ formula. For the trip to work, $d_1 = 60t_1$, where d_1 is the distance to work and t_1 is the time to drive to work. For the trip home, $d_2 = 80t_2$, where d_2 is the distance to home and t_2 is the time to drive home. To calculate the average speed, divide the total distance by the total time: $\dfrac{d_1+d_2}{t_1+t_2}$. Next, we'll substitute in the expressions that we wrote for the two distances in terms of the times and set the expression

for the average speed to 70, the average speed given in the problem.

$$\frac{d_1 + d_2}{t_1 + t_2} = \frac{60t_1 + 80t_2}{t_1 + t_2} = 70$$

Now, cross-multiply to find that $60t_1 + 80t_2 = 70t_1 + 70t_2$. Collecting like terms, we get $10t_2 = 10t_1$. Finally, dividing both sides by 10 shows that $t_2 = t_1$.

Our intuition about the symmetry for the times was correct! Now, however, we know that we aren't making an assumption. Rather, we are using a property of averages to conclude that the times for each leg of the journey are the same.

You may be thinking that there's no way that there's time to do all of that on the test. You're right about that! You wouldn't do all that work on the test to prove that the times are the same. However, it was worthwhile doing here so that we can recognize when the times would be the same and when they wouldn't, should there be a problem like this one on the test.

Now, here's what you'd actually do if you got this problem on the test.

Note that the average speed is equal to the average of the two speeds

for each leg of the journey. That means that the weight of each speed

must be the same in the calculation of the average speed. Because

the distances for each leg of the journey are different, the only way to

achieve this equal weighting for the two different speeds is if the time

spent driving each leg is the same. Therefore, the time for each part of

the trip is $\frac{3}{4}$ hour. Using the formula $d = rt$, the distance for the trip

home is $d = (80)\left(\frac{3}{4}\right) = 60$. The correct answer is (B).

Using Symmetry with Repeated Calculations

The length of a rectangle with area x is four times its width. If the vertices of an inscribed parallelogram are the midpoints of the sides of the rectangle, which of the following is an expression for the perimeter of the parallelogram?

(A) $\sqrt{17x}$

(B) $2\sqrt{17x}$

(C) $4\sqrt{17x}$

(D) $\dfrac{\sqrt{x}}{2}$

(E) $\dfrac{\sqrt{x}}{4}$

Solution 1: Sometimes the test-writers provide a figure. Sometimes they don't! This problem falls into the latter category. To turn the tables on the test-writers, we'll draw our own figure. We'll start by drawing a rectangle because working in bite-sized pieces is always a good idea!

Two notes about this figure. First, the problem describes a rectangle for which one side is four times the length of the other side. We don't need to worry too much about the scale, but we also want to avoid drawing a square! Second, we've labeled the vertices of this rectangle. You don't need to do that for your figure. We only added the labels to make it easier to refer to specific sides in the rest of this explanation.

Now we need to add the parallelogram. The problem tells us that the vertices are the midpoints of each side. We'll start by adding a dot to represent the midpoint of each side and then connect the dots.[8] Again, we're going to add labels to each of these midpoints so that we can more easily refer to them in this explanation. You can consider such labels optional in your figure. Here's the finished figure:

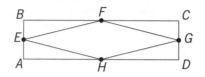

Now that we have a figure, we can get proceed with the solution. We need to find the perimeter of the parallelogram, so we need to find the lengths of its side, which are *EF*, *FG*, *GH*, and *EH*, in the figure above. But how many separate calculations do we need to do? Are any of the sides equal?

Answering those questions is how symmetry helps us out on this problem. We'll start by noting that the figure is clearly symmetrical. Next, we can note that there are four right triangular regions that are each bounded by two sides of the rectangle and one side of the parallelogram. These triangles are *EBF*, *FCG*, *GDH*, and *HAE*. These regions certainly look the same in our figure, but one must always be leery of assumptions in geometry problems. Assumptions are the cause of many mistakes for geometry problems!

Let's take a better look at the two sides of each triangle that are part of the rectangle. Each triangle has one side that is half the shorter side of the rectangle. Because points *E* and *G* are the midpoints of sides *BA* and *CD*, we can conclude that *BE* = *CG* = *GD* = *AE*. Similar reasoning allows us to conclude that *BF* = *FC* = *AH* = *HD*. Because the hypotenuse of each right triangle is calculated from the lengths of the legs (or sides) of the triangle, we can conclude that the hypotenuses of the triangles have equal lengths: *EF* = *FG* = *GH* = *EH*. So, to find the perimeter of the parallelogram, we only need to find the length of one side of the parallelogram and multiply that by four.

---

[8]   The skills from kindergarten never get old!

To find the length of one of the sides of the parallelogram, we need to go back to the information that the problem provided about the rectangle. We were told that the area of the rectangle is x, and that the length of the rectangle is four times its width. We're going to need some additional variables. If we call the width w, then the length of the rectangle can be represented as $4w$.

The figure below matches up those variables to the rectangle.

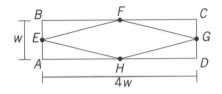

We can use these variables to find the area of the rectangle. The formula for the area of a rectangle is $A = lw$. Here, we know the area is x, and have represented the width as w and the length as $4w$. Substituting these expressions into the formula, we get $x = (4w)(w)$ or $x = 4w^2$.

You may be thinking "Why on earth would we want to do that?" Well, we're going to need our answer in terms of x, but the problem only told us about the relationship of the length to the width. So, we need a way to relate the width of the rectangle to x, the area of the rectangle. We now have an expression for x in terms of w. Let's go see how we're going to use that.

Let's focus on one of the right triangles. We'll pick EBF. In terms of w, we can represent side EB as $\frac{1}{2}w$ and side BF as $2w$. We can use the Pythagorean Theorem to find the length of the hypotenuse EF. The Pythagorean Theorem states that for any right triangle with legs of length a and b and hypotenuse of length c, $a^2 + b^2 = c^2$. Applying the Pythagorean Theorem to triangle EBF, we can state that $EF^2 = EB^2 + BF^2$. Then, using the sides expressed in terms of w, we can find that $EF^2 = \left(\frac{1}{2}w\right)^2 + (2w)^2$, or $EF^2 = \frac{1}{4}w^2 + 4w^2$. Combining like terms, we get $EF^2 = \dfrac{17}{4}w^2$. Finally, we can take the positive root[9] of both sides to find that $EF = \dfrac{w\sqrt{17}}{2}$.

Now we can find the perimeter of the parallelogram, in terms of w, by multiplying by 4: $Perimeter = 4 \times \dfrac{w\sqrt{17}}{2} = 2w\sqrt{17}$.

And that means that the correct answer is... oh, wait... the problem asked for the perimeter in terms of x and we have solved in terms of w. Don't fret! We can fix that! Let's go back to that equation that we had expressing the relationship between x and w: $x = 4w^2$. We can solve this equation for w to get $w = \dfrac{\sqrt{x}}{2}$. We can substitute this expression for w into the expression that we just found for the perimeter: $Perimeter = 2w\sqrt{17} = 2\left(\dfrac{\sqrt{x}}{2}\right)\sqrt{17} = \sqrt{x} \times \sqrt{17} = \sqrt{17x}$. Now we have an expression for the perimeter in terms of x. Note that on the last step of the substitution, we used the root rule that states that $\sqrt{m} \times \sqrt{n} = \sqrt{mn}$.

The correct answer is (A).

Solution 2: You may be thinking "Wow! That was a lot of algebra. I'm not sure I could pull that off!" Not to worry. There is another way to solve the problem. When a problem has answer choices, there's sometimes more than one way to solve it!

---

[9]   For more on arithmetic using roots, check out our bonus chapter in your online Student Tools.

In this case, we're going to solve an example of the problem. We'll use the answer we get to find the algebraic answer. We'll start by picking a number for the width of the rectangle. Let's say that $w = 2$. Now we can use the relationship stated in the problem, that the length is four times the width, to find that the length of the rectangle is 8. Then we can use the formula for the area of a rectangle, $A = lw$, to find the Area: $A = (8)(2) = 16$. The problem states that the area of the rectangle is x, so we can now set $x = 16$.

Next, we need to find the length of one side of the parallelogram. As before, we can look at one of the right triangles. Given the numbers that we used for the side lengths of the rectangle, the sides lengths (or legs) of the right triangle are 1, half the width of the rectangle, and 4, half the length of the rectangle. Then, we use the Pythagorean Theorem to find that the hypotenuse of the right triangle, which is also the side of the parallelogram, is $\sqrt{1^2 + 4^2} = \sqrt{17}$. Therefore, the perimeter of the parallelogram is $4\sqrt{17}$.

Our task now is to find which answer evaluates to $4\sqrt{17}$ when $x = 16$. Only (A) evaluates to the desired result. The answer is (A).

In effect, we used the fact that the person who wrote the problem had to do the algebra to help us out with this second solution. We didn't need to start from scratch when answering the question. It's helpful to remember that the answer choices are part of the problem!

CHAPTER 6

What to Do

Translate from Words to Symbols

Mathematics has used symbols for almost as long as mathematics has existed. Humans are a language-driven species. As such, some of the earliest mathematical ideas may have been expressed using only words. For example, simple addition with natural numbers can be expressed using only words.

However, as mathematics became more complex, there was a need for the precision that could only be attained by the use of specialized symbols to represent mathematical ideas. One of the key benefits of symbols is that symbols can be manipulated more easily than words. So, the use of symbols to express operations became an important tool for solving problems, even if those problems were often stated using words. Eventually, symbols evolved into an agreed-upon notation that could be used to express mathematical ideas.

In some small way, the GMAT and GRE expect you to recapture that history! Some problems are stated using words. However, to solve those problems, you'll find it helpful to translate those words into symbols so that those symbols can be manipulated. In this way, the test-writers are seeking to determine whether you know and can use some of the common language of mathematics. Using that common language and the precision that comes with that language is part of quantitative reasoning.

Ready for some examples? Great! Let's go translate!

Start with a Simpler Example

Two different points on the number line are both 5 units from the point with coordinate -3. The solution to which of the following equations gives the coordinates of both points?

(A) $|x+3| = 5$

(B) $|x-3| = 5$

(C) $|x|+3 = 5$

(D) $|x+5| = 3$

(E) $|x-5| = 3$

Solution 1: Write an equation that includes absolute values! Writing a regular old equation is already a daunting task! Those test-writers!

Before we get started on writing the equation, let's do a quick review of absolute values and absolute value equations. Absolute value is a measure of distance from zero on the number line. For example, $|2|$ and $|-2|$ are both equal to 2 because both 2 and -2 are a distance of 2 from 0 on the number line. The absolute value is defined for all real numbers. For example, $\left|-\dfrac{5}{2}\right| = \dfrac{5}{2}$, $\left|\sqrt{2}\right| = \sqrt{2}$, and $|0| = 0$. It's not possible to have a negative distance, so taking the absolute value of a number produces a nonnegative result.

The simplest form of an absolute value equation includes only a variable enclosed in the absolute value bars set equal to a nonnegative number. For example, $|x| = 2$ is an absolute value equation of this form. To solve this equation, it's important to understand how to interpret this equation.[1] This equation is asking us to find the two numbers that are a distance of 2 units from 0 on the number line. Hence, the solution to this equation is $x = 2$ and $x = -2$. Almost all absolute value equations of this form have two solutions because there are 2 numbers, one positive and one negative, that are a given distance from zero on the number line. The exception is the equation $|x| = 0$, which has only one solution, because only 0 is a distance of 0 from 0 on the number line.[2]

This simple form of the absolute value equation tells us the first thing that we need to know for the solution to our problem. In the equation $|x| = 2$, the number to the right of the equals sign, 2, in this case, represents the distance with which we are concerned. So, if we wanted to write an equation to find all the numbers that are a distance of three units from zero on the number line, we'd write the equation $|x| = 3$. Because distances must be nonnegative, the number that an absolute value equation of this form equals must also be nonnegative. In other words, $|x| = -3$ has no solutions because no numbers are a distance of -3 units from zero on the number line.

---

[1] Yes, equations can have interpretations!
[2] That's a lot of zeros in one sentence!

What if we were interested in finding the two numbers that are a given distance from a number other than zero? Could we use an absolute value equation to find those numbers? Yes! To see how, let's rewrite our sample equation, $|x| = 2$, as $|x + 0| = 2$. Clearly, this form of the equation doesn't change the solution. However, it does help us to focus on how we can incorporate the number from which we want to find the distance into the equation.

For example, let's look at this equation: $|x + 1| = 2$. We'll proceed by first solving the equation and then assessing the effect of adding 1 to x inside the absolute value bars. To solve the equation, it's important to note that the expression inside the absolute value bars could be either 2 or -2 to produce an absolute value of 2. So, we'll set the expression inside the absolute value bars to both 2 and -2 and solve both equations. If $x + 1 = 2$, then $x = 1$. If $x + 1 = -2$, then $x = -3$. Both these solutions, 1 and -3, are a distance of two units from -1 on the number line. So, adding 1 to x essentially shifted our starting number, 1, to the left of 0 on the number line. Put another way, this equation can be used to find the two numbers that are a distance of two units from -1 on the number line. Similar reasoning enables us to conclude that the equation $|x - 1| = 2$, which has solutions -1 and 3, can be used to find the two numbers that are a distance of two units from 1 on the line.

There are other things that we could do to our equation, such as making the coefficient of x something other than 1. Or, we could add or subtract a number to the absolute value expression. However, we have what we need to solve our problem.

Now that we understand the different parts of an absolute value equation, here's the condensed explanation.

Note that the question asks for the two numbers that are a distance of five units from -3 on the number line. The reference to two solutions indicates that we can use an absolute value equation to solve. In an absolute value equation, the number representing the distance goes on one side of the equals sign. The number representing the starting point from which to calculate the distance goes inside the absolute value bars and is either added or subtracted from the variable. In this case, the starting number is -3, so add 3 to the variable. The equation is $|x + 3| = 5$. The correct answer is (A).

Solution 2: Of course, we can also take advantage of the fact that answers are provided. The person who wrote the problem had to know how to write the equation, so we can piggyback our work off that person's work.

The problem states that we need two numbers that are a distance of five from −3 on the number line. We can find one such number by adding 5 to −3 to get −3 + 5 = 2. We can find the other number by subtracting 5 from −3 to get −3 − 5 = −8. These two numbers represent the solutions to the desired equation. We can find the right equation in the answers by plugging these solutions into the answers.

If $x = 2$, then the equations in (A), (C), and (E) are true. Eliminate (B) and (D). Now, use $x = -8$ to check the remaining answer choices. Only (A) is true when $x = -8$. The correct answer is (A).

It's always helpful to think about different ways to solve a problem! It's also helpful to remember that there are often ways to use the answer choices when solving a problem.

Translating Math Terms

Which of the following is the difference when $\frac{1}{5}$ percent of 2,000 is subtracted from $\frac{1}{5}$ of 2,000 ?

(A)   0
(B)   40
(C)   360
(D)   396
(E)   400

Solution: Oh sure, the test-writers could give you the expressions and this problem would still present some challenges. But you may have noticed that the test-writers don't do a lot of favors for the test-takers! So, here's a classic case of a problem that is made more difficult because it requires the test-taker to translate the words into math symbols to solve.

The test-writers have also raised the difficulty by making it easy to mis-read the problem. One of the most common causes of errors on either the GMAT or GRE is misreading a problem. For test-takers who read this problem too fast, the groups of words may sound the same, so they pick (A), 0, as their answer. For either the GMAT or GRE, if you get an answer very quickly and have done little or no work to get that answer, you should reread the question. You may be about to fall for a trap. Put another way, the test-writers aren't likely to let you go to a good grad or business school for doing anything too easy!

Let's get to work translating the different groups of words in this prob-

lem into math symbols. We can start with the first group of words: $\frac{1}{5}$

percent of 2,000. The first word that we need to know how to translate

is *percent*. Percent means out of 100. So, whatever number comes

before the word percent goes over 100. That's straightforward if the

number is something like 10, and we could say that the translation of

10 percent is $\frac{10}{100}$. Here, the test-writers are trying to confuse us by

using a weirder number, but we're not going to let that throw us. We're

just going to put $\frac{1}{5}$ over 100 to get $\frac{\left(\frac{1}{5}\right)}{100}$. Next, we see the word *of*.

In word problems, *of* translates as multiply. So, we're going to find the

product of $\frac{\left(\frac{1}{5}\right)}{100}$ and 2,000. The first group of words translates as

$$\frac{\left(\frac{1}{5}\right)}{100} \times 2,000$$

We can then use what is called the dropdown rule[3] for fractions that have fractions as their numerators to clean up the fraction and then evaluate the expression:

$$\frac{\left(\dfrac{1}{5}\right)}{100} \times 2,000 = \frac{1}{(5)(100)} \times 2,000 = \frac{1}{500} \times 2,000 = 4$$

Now that we know that the first group of words evaluates to 4, we can turn our attention to the second group of words. This grouping is easier. The word *of* tells us that we are going to multiply $\dfrac{1}{5}$ by 2,000. So, this group translates to $\dfrac{1}{5} \times 2,000$ and evaluates to $\dfrac{1}{5} \times 2,000 = 400$.

Now, we just need to deal with the subtraction. The answer choices can guide us about which number to subtract from which, or we can replace the groups of words with the numbers that we found when we evaluated each group of words. So, we are being asked for "the difference when 4 is subtracted from 400." Phrased that way, we can see that 400 − 4 = 396 gives us the answer. The correct answer is (D).

Translating in Bite-Sized Pieces

A group of 10 roommates share the rent for an apartment equally. If the apartment's monthly rent is r dollars and x of the roommates move out, which of the following is an expression for the additional rent paid by each remaining roommate?

(A) $\dfrac{rx}{10(10-x)}$

(B) $\dfrac{10r}{x}$

(C) $\dfrac{r}{10(10-x)}$

(D) $\dfrac{r}{10-x}$

(E) $\dfrac{rx}{10-x}$

---

[3] For more on the dropdown rule and other information about fractions, check your online Student Tools.

Solution 1: Let's hear it for the classic algebra word problem. You can't have a standardized test without one! It's a rule. Or at least, it certainly seems like it's a rule.

The key to solving a word problem that requires writing an algebraic expression is to work in bite-sized pieces. Nobody looks at these problems and instantly knows the full expression. Instead, each piece of the problem is translated. It's also often necessary to do some algebraic manipulation to make the translation match one of the answer choices.

Most of these problems are written in a very linear way. So, the information that you need first is at the beginning of the problem. The information that you need last is at the end of the problem. In most cases, you need to use all the information in the problem. So, if your expression doesn't match one of the answer choices, it's likely that you inadvertently skipped over some information.

This problem starts by telling us that there are 10 roommates and that they share the rent equally. We need to keep that in mind, but we can't translate anything based on only the first sentence. However, the next sentence tells us that the rent is r dollars. Now that we know the rent, we can use the information from the first sentence to write an expression for the rent paid by each roommate. To do that, we just need to divide the total rent, r, by the number of roommates. So, each roommate pays $\dfrac{r}{10}$ dollars.

Next, the problem tells us that x of the roommates move out. That means that the remaining roommates still need to pay the full rent because, you know, landlords. We can write an expression for how much rent each remaining roommate now pays. To do that, we need to express the number of remaining roommates using the variable x, the number of roommates who move out. To do that, we just subtract x from 10, the original number of roommates, to get $10 - x$. Each of our $10 - x$ remaining roommates pays an equal share of the rent. So, we can find the rent paid by each remaining roommate by dividing the total rent, r, by the number of remaining roommates, $10 - x$, to get $\dfrac{r}{10 - x}$.

Now we need to pay attention to the question posed by the problem. We need an expression for the additional rent paid by each remaining roommate. To find that, we need to subtract the original amount paid by each roommate, $\dfrac{r}{10}$, from the new, higher amount paid by each remaining roommate, $\dfrac{r}{10 - x}$. That give us this expression: $\dfrac{r}{10 - x} - \dfrac{r}{10}$.

We might eagerly look at the answers thinking that we're done and can move to the next problem. Alas, none of the answers match our expression. Does that mean that we made a mistake? Not necessarily. The test-writers may have decided that they wanted the answer in a different form. Note that none of the answer choices include more than one fraction. It looks like we need to complete the subtraction[4] to make our answer look like one of the answer choices.

To subtract (or add) two fractions, we need a common denominator. When dealing with algebraic expressions, the easiest way to do that is to multiply the expressions (or numbers) in the denominators. Here, that means that our common denominator is $10(10 - x)$. We are very purposefully going to not distribute the 10. By leaving the common denominator in this undistributed form, it will make it easier for us to adjust the numerators. We need to adjust the numerators because we don't want to change the value of the fractions. For example, $\dfrac{r}{10 - x} \neq \dfrac{r}{10(10 - x)}$. However, for the first fraction, if we multiply the numerator by 10, we won't change the value. For the second fraction, we multiply the numerator by $10 - x$. Here's what our subtraction problem looks like now:

$$\frac{10r}{10(10 - x)} - \frac{r(10 - x)}{10(10 - x)}$$

---

[4] For more on fraction arithmetic, check out the bonus chapter in your online Student Tools.

Note that we can cancel terms in both fractions to get the original form of our subtraction problem. We just need to perform a few more steps to get our expression to look like one of the answer choices. We'll start by just combining the two fractions into one fraction. Because we have a common denominator, we can just show the subtraction in the numerators:

$$\frac{10r - r(10 - x)}{10(10 - x)}$$

Next, we'll distribute the r in the second expression in the numerator:

$$\frac{10r - 10r + rx}{10(10 - x)}$$

Now we just need to clean up the numerator. Note that we are subtracting $10r$ from $10r$, so those terms drop out.

Our final expression is:

$$\frac{rx}{10(10 - x)}$$

The correct answer is (A).

Solution 2: Now that we've looked at how to write the expression to solve the problem, let's talk about whether we need to solve the problem that way. You may have already noticed that a lot of the answers look very similar. That's because the test-writers spent some time thinking about some of the common algebraic mistakes that someone might make when solving the problem. Test-writers spend a lot of time thinking about how people make mistakes. They know that if they can populate the answer choices with answers based on common mistakes, they can raise the difficulty level of the problem. As though they needed to raise the difficulty level of this problem!

So, if we solve the problem as the test-writers expect, using all that lovely algebra in the previous solution, we could make a mistake and never know it. Is there any other way to solve the problem?

Would I have asked the question if there weren't? Here's another place where we can remember that the person who wrote the problem also had to solve the problem. That person did the algebra. We can again piggyback our work off that person's work.

How do we do that? Algebra provides a general solution to a problem. Here, we came up with an expression that we could use to find the additional rent for any values of r and x that we plugged in. We could even make the formula cover a more general situation where there are y roommates at the beginning rather than 10. But we already have 5 possibilities for the correct general solution. We just need to find the one that works.

Remember back in school when you learned algebra? You were told to check your work by putting a number into your expression. We're going to do the same thing. We're going to solve an example of the problem by replacing the variables in the problem with numbers. Then, we'll see which answer choice matches our numerical answer to our example of the problem.

Let's say that we make r, the rent, equal to $100. That means that each of the 10 roommates is originally paying $10 in rent.[5] Now, let's have 5 roommates move out, so $x = 5$. Now each of the remaining 5 roommates needs to kick in $20 to pay the rent. So, the additional rent paid by each remaining roommate is $20 − $10 − $10.

We need to find the answer that yields 10 when $r = 100$ and $x = 5$. It's good form to check all the answer choices when solving problems in this way, just to make sure that only one answer matches the numerical answer to the problem. In this case, only (A) equals 10. The correct answer is (A).

---

[5] Nobody said our numbers needed to be realistic!

Where to Begin Translating

When the reciprocal of the square of a certain positive integer is multiplied by 16, the positive square root of the resulting number is equal to the result of moving the decimal point of the original number two places to the left. What is the original number?

(A) 2
(B) 4
(C) 20
(D) 40
(E) 400

Solution: Yikes, that's a lot of words! The test-writers have certainly gone out of their way to make this problem sound as complicated as possible. The key to dealing with a problem such as this one is to work in bite-sized pieces. Don't try to translate everything at once!

One of the challenges of this problem is deciding where to begin translating. There are two rules of thumb that apply to that decision. First, in most cases, start close to the beginning of the problem. Second, look for a group of words that seems at least somewhat straightforward.

For this problem, a good starting point is the phrase "the square of a certain positive integer." We are going to write an equation, so we'll need a variable. We can represent the "certain positive integer," an unknown that we are solving for, with the variable x. Next, we need to consider "the square" of that integer, so we'll square our variable to get x^2.

We need to be careful about the context. We might be tempted to multiply x^2 by 16, but if we read from the beginning, we see that it is the reciprocal of x^2 that gets multiplied by 16. The reciprocal of x^2 is $\dfrac{1}{x^2}$.[6] Now we can multiply the reciprocal by 16 to get $\dfrac{16}{x^2}$. So far, so good!

---

[6] Recall that the product of a number or expression and its reciprocal is 1. In this case, the reciprocal of x^2 is $\dfrac{1}{x^2}$ because $\left(x^2\right)\left(\dfrac{1}{x^2}\right)=1$. Note that we could get fancy and represent the reciprocal using a negative exponent, but we'll eschew the need to get fancy! However, if you want more of that fancy stuff, check out our bonus chapter in your online Student Tools.

Next, we encounter the phrase "the positive square root of the resulting number." The resulting number is the expression that we just found, $\frac{16}{x^2}$. We need to take the square root of that number. So, that's $\sqrt{\frac{16}{x^2}}$. There isn't a way to indicate that we only want the positive root, so we'll need to remember that once we get the full equation and start to solve.

The next group of words, "is equal to," are reasonably straightforward. We're going to put an equals sign after the square root expression that we just found. But, we're going to set the expression equal to "the result of moving the decimal point of the original number two places to the left." What does that mean, and how do we represent it?

Sometimes, it helps to think about an example. Suppose that we started with an easy number, such as 10. We'll write this number as 10.0 so that we can see where the decimal point currently is. We're supposed to move the decimal point two places to the left. That will give us 0.10. Each time that we moved the decimal point one place to the left was equivalent to dividing by 10. So, to get from 10.0 to 0.10, we divided by $10 \times 10 = 100$. We can take that same approach to translate the wording in the problem. To move the decimal point for our original number, x, two places to the left, we need to divide by 100. We'll represent that by $\frac{x}{100}$. We can set the two expressions equal:

$$\sqrt{\frac{16}{x^2}} = \frac{x}{100}$$

Now we just need to solve. We can start by taking the square root of the expression on the left side of the equation. The rule for taking the square root of a fraction is $\sqrt{\frac{n}{m}} = \frac{\sqrt{n}}{\sqrt{m}}$. So, we just need to take the square root of the numerator and the denominator. The denominator is the reason that the problem stated that we want the positive root. It's also helpful to remember that squaring a number and taking its square root are inverse operations. Here's what we get after taking the square root:

$$\frac{4}{x} = \frac{x}{100}$$

Now we have a fraction on both sides of the equals sign. That's a job for cross-multiplying! After cross-multiplying, we get $x^2 = 400$. Finally, take the (positive) square root of both sides to find that $x = 20$. The correct answer is (C).

Apply Properties and Formulas to New Situations

What mathematician doesn't love a good generalization? Seeking ever more general solutions is one of the reasons that mathematicians get out of bed in the morning. Seriously, it's true!

Neither the GMAT nor the GRE expects you to go that far down the generalization path. However, the test-writers do want to see whether you can apply properties and formulas to new—or at least less frequently encountered—situations.

What constitutes a new or less frequently tested situation? One example might be calculating the area of a circle that has an unusual radius, such as $\sqrt{2}$.[7] Another might be applying a definition to an unusual situation, such as finding the remainder when 4 is divided by 6.[8] In both cases, these calculations involve twists on concepts with which many test-takers feel comfortable.

---

[7] The area is $A = \pi\left(\sqrt{2}\right)^2 = 2\pi$.

[8] The remainder is 4. For two positive integers, a and b, if $a < b$, then the remainder when a is divided by b is a.

There's also the issue of being able to determine the concept being tested. Some problems on both the GMAT and the GRE test routine concepts in unusual ways. For such problems, it's actually important to know the content areas tested by each exam. Why? Because it's much more common for a routine concept to be tested in an unusual way than for an unusual concept to be tested in a routine way on a standardized test. After all, standardized tests need to test standard content. So, sometimes you need to stop and take stock of the clues in a question that help you to determine the concept being tested.

And, of course, there's algebra. Part of the point of algebra is to find more general solutions to situations. Why know that Ben is 20 years old and that Jack is five years older than Ben, when we can say that Ben is *b* years old and that Jack is five years older than Ben so we can come up with an expression for Jack's age in terms of *b*? (It's *b* + 5, by the way!) Now we have an expression that can be used to find Jack's age for any age that we make Ben.

Let's take a look at some problems that test some routine concepts in ways that you may not have used them before.

When Numbers Get Weird

What is the percent increase from $\sqrt{4^{-3}}$ to

$\sqrt[3]{8^{-2}}$?

(A) 12.5%
(B) 25%
(C) 50%
(D) 100%
(E) 200%

Solution: The first part of this problem doesn't seem too bad. The setup is just to calculate a percent increase. But then the problem goes off the rails, doesn't it? Rather than asking about a percent increase from a nice number such as 5 to another nice number such as 10, the problem uses some pretty crazy-looking numbers.

Here's the thing, though. Remember when we said that it's good practice to get comfortable using different kinds of numbers in formulas?

This is why. Formulas still work, even when the numbers aren't nice. The test-writers are hoping that you'll panic and give up when you see the crazy numbers. But we're not going to fall for that, are we?

First things first, let's review how to find a percent change. Here's a formula that we can use:

$$\text{percent change} = \frac{\text{difference}}{\text{original}} \times 100$$

There are a couple of things to know about how this formula applies to the GMAT or GRE. Neither test ever asks for a percent change because the test-writers evidently have an aversion to including negative percentages in the answer choices. Instead, the question will ask for a percent increase or a percent decrease. Why does that matter? It means that the difference in the formula is always the positive difference between the two numbers in the problem.

It's usually easy to determine which number is the original. Some problems use time references such as years or months. Other problems use the words *from* and *to*, with *from* indicating the original. Still others actually use a word such as *original* or *originally*. When those clues are absent, which number is the original is determined by whether the question asks for a percent increase or percent decrease.[9] If the question asks for a percent increase, the original is the smaller number. If the question asks for a percent decrease, the original is the larger number.

Remember that neither the GMAT nor the GRE really cares that much about your calculating ability. So, there's a good chance that the numbers used in this problem evaluate to numbers that are easier to work with. By using these strange numbers, the test-writers get to test more than whether you just know how to calculate a percent increase. They also get to test your ability to work with roots and exponents. And they get to test whether you can use a formula in a more general way. Remember that mathematicians love to generalize!

---

[9] There are some related phrasings that are also used. Percent increase is sometimes phrased as *percent greater* or *percent more*. Percent decrease is sometimes phrased as *percent less*.

So, let's take a look at those numbers,[10] starting with $\sqrt{4^{-3}}$. We can start by rewriting the number under the radical. To do so, we need to use the definition of a negative exponent: for all $x \neq 0$, $x^{-n} = \dfrac{1}{x^n}$. So, we can rewrite $\sqrt{4^{-3}}$ as $\sqrt{\dfrac{1}{4^3}} = \sqrt{\dfrac{1}{64}}$. Next, we can take the square root of the fraction. To take the square root of a fraction, take the square root of the numerator and the denominator. So, $\sqrt{\dfrac{1}{64}} = \dfrac{\sqrt{1}}{\sqrt{64}} = \dfrac{1}{8}$. As suspected, the first number evaluates to a much nicer number.

Now, let's evaluate the second number. We'll start in the same way, by using the definition of a negative exponent: $\sqrt[3]{8^{-2}} = \sqrt[3]{\dfrac{1}{8^2}} = \sqrt[3]{\dfrac{1}{64}}$. In the same way that we find the square root of a fraction by taking the square root of the numerator and denominator, we find the cube root of a fraction by taking the cube root of the numerator and denominator. So, $\sqrt[3]{\dfrac{1}{64}} = \dfrac{\sqrt[3]{1}}{\sqrt[3]{64}} = \dfrac{1}{4}$. The second number also evaluates to a much nicer number.

We can now restate the question using the nicer numbers: what is the percent increase from $\dfrac{1}{8}$ to $\dfrac{1}{4}$?

We can put those numbers into the formula:

$$\text{percent increase} = \dfrac{\left(\dfrac{1}{4} - \dfrac{1}{8}\right)}{\left(\dfrac{1}{8}\right)} \times 100$$

---

[10] For more on arithmetic with roots and exponents, check out our bonus chapter in your online Student Tools.

Then, subtract the fractions in the numerator:

$$\text{percent increase} = \frac{\left(\dfrac{1}{8}\right)}{\left(\dfrac{1}{8}\right)} \times 100$$

The fractions in the numerator and denominator cancel, so the percent increase is 100%. The correct answer is (D).

Know What the Test-Writers Like to Test

In an increasing sequence of 10 consecutive even integers, the sum of the last 5 integers is 670. What is the sum of the first 5 integers in the sequence?

(A) 620
(B) 645
(C) 660
(D) 665
(E) 720

Solution 1: Um, test-writers? Hello? You didn't tell us what the numbers are, so how are we supposed to find the sum of the first 5 integers when all we know is the sum of the last 5 integers?

When encountering a novel situation, many test-takers start to think about some of the most unusual math they've ever learned. That's understandable. However, it's important to remember that the GMAT and GRE are testing quantitative reasoning ability rather than knowledge of math per se. So, it's much more likely that a commonly tested topic is being tested in an unusual way than that an unusual topic is being tested in the usual way. In other words, there's power in knowing what the GMAT and GRE like to test! When you encounter an unusual situation, take a moment to look for clues that could link that situation back to topics that you've seen in other problems.

For this problem, we can note that the terms of the sequence are con-secutive even integers. Next, the problem refers to the sum of the last 5 integers. So, we know the sum and that there are 5 integers. The sum and the number of integers means that we have two of the variables used in the formula for an average or arithmetic mean. The problem may not have explicitly used the term *average* or *arithmetic mean*, but this question is testing the concept of averages.[11]

The average (arithmetic mean) of the last five integers is $670 \div 5 = 134$. We can make use of the fact that the numbers in the sequence are consecutive even numbers. When numbers in a list are evenly spaced, the average and the median are equal. *Evenly spaced* just means that the distance between each term in the sequence is the same. Here, because the terms are even numbers, each term is a distance of 2 from the term that immediately proceeds it, so the terms are evenly spaced. Hence, 134 is both the average and the median of the five numbers. If 134 is the median of the last five numbers, it is the eighth term in the sequence.[12]

We could just work backwards from the eighth term to write out the val-ues of the first through fifth terms at this point and then find the sum of the values of those terms. However, we don't really need the values of all the terms. The third term is the median and hence, the average of the first five numbers. So, we can just work backwards to find that the value of the third term is 124. Now we have the average and the number of terms, so we can multiply to find that the sum of the first five numbers is $5 \times 124 = 620$. The correct answer is (A).

Solution 2: Ready for a more idiosyncratic approach? Quantitative rea-soning sometimes involves matching up items that play similar roles. In this sequence, we can match up the first term with the sixth term, the second term with the seventh term, the third term with the eighth term, the fourth term with the ninth term, and the fifth term with the tenth term. Why would we want to do that?

Well, consider this sequence of ten consecutive even integers: 2, 4, 6, 8, 10, 12, 14, 16, 18, 20. Now, note the relationship between the terms that we paired up. The sixth term is 10 more than the first term. The seventh term is 10 more than the second term. And so on.

---

[11] For more information on averages, medians, and other descriptive statistics, check out our bonus chapter in your online Student Tools.

[12] The last five numbers are the 6th, 7th, 8th, 9th, and 10th terms in the sequence. The 8th term is the middle term so it is the median.

That means that the sum of the last five numbers is 50 more than the sum of the first five numbers. Therefore, the sum of the first five numbers is $670 - 50 = 620$. The correct answer is (A).

Is this way a better way to solve the problem? Well, it is a little faster. However, it's only faster if you happen to think about it very soon after you read the problem!

Many problems on the GMAT or GRE can be solved in idiosyncratic ways. However, you don't get any extra credit for solving the problem in one of these ways. If you see an idiosyncratic way to solve a problem as soon as you finish reading it, it's okay to take advantage of that. However, it may take more time to find the "faster" way than to simply get to work solving the problem in a way that has more steps.

When Equations Get Weird

If $x^{-2} + 2x^{-1} = 15$, which of the following could be the value of x ?

(A) -5

(B) $-\dfrac{1}{5}$

(C) $-\dfrac{1}{3}$

(D) 3

(E) 5

Solution 1: Negative exponents in an equation? Is that allowed? So, more things in heaven and earth and all that. It's a theme with math. Push the limits. Make things more general. So, yeah, negative exponents in an equation are allowed! However, the test-writers are counting on the fact that you may not have seen an equation that looks like this one before. Or, if you have seen such an equation, it was a long time ago.

So, what to do with those negative exponents? How do we solve an equation that looks like this one?

Well, one solution is to avoid solving the equation. The person who wrote the problem had to solve the equation, so we can take advantage of that person's work. To do so, we can just test out the answers until we find the one that works. Sometimes it's important to remember that the inclusion of answer choices often means that there are additional ways to solve the problem.

Notice that the answer choices are in numerically ascending order. Test-writers have quirks. They like to put answers in order. We're going to take advantage of that and start with (C). If (C) works, we're done. If it doesn't, we may know whether we need a bigger or smaller number.

The values in the answer choices are possible values of x. So, we'll substitute the value in (C) into the equation for x and evaluate. Doing that gives us $\left(-\dfrac{1}{3}\right)^{-2} + 2\left(-\dfrac{1}{3}\right)^{-1}$ on the left side of the equation. We'll use the definition of a negative exponent, $x^{-n} = \dfrac{1}{x^n}$, to evaluate.

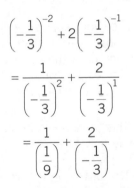

$$\left(-\frac{1}{3}\right)^{-2} + 2\left(-\frac{1}{3}\right)^{-1}$$

$$= \frac{1}{\left(-\dfrac{1}{3}\right)^2} + \frac{2}{\left(-\dfrac{1}{3}\right)^1}$$

$$= \frac{1}{\left(\dfrac{1}{9}\right)} + \frac{2}{\left(-\dfrac{1}{3}\right)}$$

For the last step, we evaluated the exponents for each denominator. Now we have two fractions that have fractions as their denominators. That's a perfect opportunity to use what is called the roll up rule[13] for fractions to get $9 - (2)(3) = 3$. Of course, to make the equation true, we should have gotten 15. So, (C) is incorrect and can be eliminated.

It's hard to tell if we need a bigger number or a smaller number. However, we can notice that three of the remaining answers are integers while one answer is a fraction. So, it does make sense to ask whether the answer is more likely to be an integer or a fraction. For that, we need to

---

[13] For more on the roll up rule and other information about fractions, check your online Student Tools.

remember that negative exponents are ways of writing reciprocals. So, if we apply a negative exponent[14] to an integer, we'll get a fraction as a result. Since we want the sum of the two terms with negative exponents in our equation to be 15, it seems unlikely that we'd achieve that by adding two fractions. Let's try the other fraction:

$$\left(-\frac{1}{5}\right)^{-2} + 2\left(-\frac{1}{5}\right)^{-1}$$

$$= \frac{1}{\left(-\dfrac{1}{5}\right)^{2}} + \frac{2}{\left(-\dfrac{1}{5}\right)^{1}}$$

$$= \frac{1}{\left(\dfrac{1}{25}\right)} + \frac{2}{\left(-\dfrac{1}{5}\right)}$$

Using the roll up rule, we get $25 - (2)(5) = 25 - 10 = 15$. That's what we wanted! So, the correct answer is (B).

Solution 2: Yeah, but how do you really solve it? First off, we did really solve the problem. Remember that all that matters on a test such as the GMAT or GRE is that you click the correct bubble. The test-writers award the same credit to the person who made a lucky guess as to the person who produced the most elegant solution.[15]

So, let's talk about why this problem is in our section about applying properties[16] and formulas to new situations.

Let's start by moving 15 to the left side of the equation to get $x^{-2} + 2x^{-1} - 15 = 0$. Is the equation starting to look more familiar now? If only those exponents were positive, the equation would be a quadratic equation. There are sufficient similarities that we can also solve this equation by factoring.

---

[14] For more on the rules of exponents, check out our bonus chapter in your online Student Tools.

[15] Mathematicians prize elegance. When I was in college, I took an advanced course in abstract algebra. In a course like that, exam questions usually ask you to produce proofs of results. The final exam was a take-home test. For one of the questions, I could only think of what's known as a proof by exclusion. The idea is that you list out everything that can happen, systematically prove that none of those things can happen, and hence show that something is impossible. After 6 pages of work, my professor wrote "Proof completely correct. Not elegant. No credit." I'm scarred to this day. Be thankful that neither the GMAT nor the GRE award points based on the elegance of your solution to the problem!

[16] For more information on algebraic properties of exponents, check out our bonus chapter in your online Student Tools.

In your mathematical education, you've probably factored a few hundred quadratic equations. But, you probably haven't factored an equation with negative exponents. Not to fear! The process is the same. When we factor a quadratic, we usually start by writing two sets of parentheses and putting an x in each. We do that because when we FOIL,[17] we start by multiplying the two first terms. For a quadratic for which the first term is x^2, we produce x^2 by multiplying x by itself.

In this case, we want to get x^{-2} as the product of the first terms. Remember that we add the exponents when multiplying quantities with like bases, so we can see that multiplying (x^{-1}) (x^{-1}) achieves our desired result. Then, we need to find a pair of factors of 15 that have a sum or difference of 2. So, the pair that we want is 3 and 5. Putting it all together, we can factor the equation to get:

$$(x^{-1} - 3)(x^{-1} + 5) = 0$$

To have a product of 0, one or both factors must equal 0. So, we set each factor equal to 0 and solve.

$$(x^{-1} - 3) = 0 \text{ or } (x^{-1} + 5) = 0$$
$$x^{-1} = 3 \text{ or } x^{-1} = -5$$

Now we just need to be careful. The problem didn't ask for a possible value of x^{-1} but rather the value of x. We can use the definition of a negative exponent to rewrite the solutions as:

$$\frac{1}{x} = 3 \quad \text{or} \quad \frac{1}{x} = -5$$

We can solve for x by taking the reciprocal of both sides of each equation to find that $x = \frac{1}{3}$ or $x = -\frac{1}{5}$. Choice (B) matches one of these solutions.

---

[17] FOIL is the process for multiplying two binomial expressions. You probably remember that the acronym stands for Firsts, Outsides, Insides, Lasts. For example, to multiply $(x + 3)(x + 2)$, multiply the first terms to get $(x)(x) = x^2$. Then multiply the outside terms to get $(x)(2) = 2x$. Then, the inside terms to get $(3)(x) = 3x$. Then, the outside last terms to get $(3)(2) = 6$. Then, collect like terms: $x^2 + 2x + 3x + 6 = x^2 + 5x + 6$. Factoring a quadratic is just doing the FOIL process in reverse.

But remember: there are no points for elegance on the GMAT or GRE!

Work with Abstract Concepts

Just as mathematicians prize generalization, they also prize abstraction. In fact, it's fair to say that the two guiding principles of much mathematical research are generalization and abstraction.

Again, the test-writers don't expect you to go too far down the abstraction path. However, they do want to see whether you can work with a certain level of abstraction. So, rather than ask you to find the average of 3 and 5, they might ask you to find an expression for the average of a and b.

The solution to a problem that deals with a concept in a more abstract way often requires a very firm grasp of that concept. It may also require some flexibility in the way that you think about that concept. Could those be reasons that the test-writers include such problems in the quantitative reasoning section? Um, yeah!

Here are some specific examples so that we don't leave this important skill as an abstraction.

Weird Symbols

For all positive integers greater than 1, if $a \# b$ is defined as the remainder when a is divided by b, what is the value of $4 \# (6 \# 9)$?

(A) 0
(B) 2
(C) 4
(D) 6
(E) 9

Solutions: A # symbol in the problem? Is that a typo? What new mischief have the test-writers dreamed up now?

First off, it's not a typo. Both the GMAT and the GRE will sometimes use non-standard notation in problems. These symbols are designed to get you to say "No math teacher that I've ever had told me what # means!" The test-writers are hoping that you give up.

To some extent, all notation is arbitrary. There are certain symbols, such as + and ×, that are so timeworn that they have become the standard way of expressing a mathematical operation. However, even these symbols were not always the agreed-upon convention. In the not-too-distant past, mathematicians would publish books with prefaces that explained the notation that was used in the book. In other words, each mathematician would decide the notation that would be used to express a given idea. Of course, that made reading math books harder, so eventually a lot of notation got standardized.

In a sense, problems such as this one continue this historical tradition. The test-writers just decided that they'd make up their own notation for a problem. Maybe they got bored. At any rate, just as with those math books from the past, the test-writers need to tell you what the symbols used in the problem mean.

That's the first thing to know about solving one of these problems. Don't worry that you don't recognize the notation. You weren't supposed to learn what the symbol meant before you took the test. You need to learn what the symbol means when you take the test. See—the test-writers, crafty lot that they are, are forcing you to work with an abstract concept by learning a new definition on the spot and applying it to a given situation.

So, step one is to look for a definition of the symbol. Here, the problem states that *a # b* is *defined as the remainder when a is divided by b*. The problem also tells us that this definition only applies to positive integers greater than 1. That restriction is nice to know, but all of the numbers that they give us to work with are positive integers greater than 1, so we can ignore this restriction.[18]

We do note that the definition includes the word *remainder*. So, let's do a quick refresh on finding remainders. First off, remainders are integers. When one integer, *a*, is divided by another integer, *b*, two things

---

[18] The restriction is included in the problem because of the way that remainders are usually defined. However, the restriction has no practical effect on the solution to this problem.

can happen. Either *a* is divisible by *b*, in which case the remainder is 0, or *a* is not divisible by *b*, in which case the remainder is an integer that is less than *b*. An example of the first case is 10 ÷ 5, because 10 is divisible by 5. An example of the second case is 11 ÷ 5, because 11 is not divisible by 5. So, when we divide 11 by 5, there's something left over.

How do we determine what is left over? Well, let's say that we have 11 berries and 5 people and we wish to give each person as many whole berries as possible. We start by giving each person one berry. Then, we give each person a second berry. But we only have one berry left, so we can't distribute any additional berries unless one person gets more than anyone else. So we have a remainder of 1.

That means that one way to think of a remainder is that a remainder is a measure of distance from the closest multiple of the number that we are dividing by. In our example, we were dividing by 5, and we found out that we could distribute 10 berries. Ten is the closest multiple of 5 to 11. The distance between that closest multiple of 5 to 11, which is 10, is 1. In other words, $11 \div 5 = (5)(2) + 1$, where 1 is the remainder.

Okay, let's go solve that problem. We start with the numbers in parentheses because that's what the PEMDAS convention tells us to do. So we need to find the remainder for 6 ÷ 9. Be careful! You might be tempted to think that the remainder is 0 because 6 is less than 9. However, think about the way that we wrote 11 ÷ 5. How many full times does 9 go into 6? Zero, right? What's left over? All 6 that we started with. In other words, $6 \div 9 = (9)(0) + 6$, where 6 is the remainder.

Now, insert that remainder that we just found into the problem. The part in the parentheses evaluates to 6. The problem is now 4 # 6. So, we need to find the remainder when 4 is divided by 6. The test-writers are playing the same trick again by making the number we are dividing by less than the number we are dividing into. But, we can apply the same reasoning as the reasoning we applied to 6 ÷ 9. How many full times does 6 go into 4? Zero! What's left over? All 4 that we started with! In other words, $4 \div 6 = (6)(0) + 4$, where 4 is the remainder. Hence, 4 # (6 # 9) = 4. The correct answer is (C).

Using Clues

If the product of the integers r, s, t, and u is 910, and if $1 < r < s < t < u$, what is the value of $u - s$?

(A) 2
(B) 5
(C) 7
(D) 8
(E) 11

Solution: If your first response to this question was "Where's the answer that says it could by anything?" or "Can I pick all the answers?," you're not alone! It certainly seems as though there should be more than one possible answer for this difference, doesn't it?

However, note that the question asks for *the* value of $u - s$. You can generally trust that the test-writers know their math! If they say that there is only one value, there's only one value![19]

Our strategy, in this case, is to look for clues about what the question may be testing, and there are clues aplenty in this question! First, note that 910 is the product of four integers. Even the fact that we are told that the numbers are integers is significant. Next, we're told that $1 < r < s < t < u$. While that restriction may look unimportant, it's the last clue that we need to determine the concept tested by this question. The restriction means that there are four *different* integers. None of the integers is equal to any of the other integers. We'll also see another role that this condition plays in the solution to the problem.

So, have you deduced the abstract concept that this question is testing? If you said **prime factorization**, you've got it! But there's a little more to it. The question is testing something specific about prime factorization. It's testing the **Fundamental Theorem of Arithmetic**, which states that for any positive integer greater than 1, there is a unique way to represent that integer as a product of prime numbers.[20]

---

[19] Questions for tests such as the GMAT and GRE undergo multiple rounds of expert review before they are included even as experimental questions. Expert review catches any gross errors, such as there being more than one value. Experimental testing almost always catches even subtle wording errors. It's incredibly rare for a scored question to contain any errors.

[20] Rearrangements of those **prime factors** don't count as different factorizations. For example, 2 × 3, the prime factorization of 6, is the same as 3 × 2.

So the test-writers wanted to see whether you know and can use the Fundamental Theorem of Arithmetic, but they didn't come right out and ask you to find the prime factorization of 910. They just gave you clues about the concept. In other words, they added a level of abstraction (aka difficulty!) to the question.

Okay, time to factor. The commonly used tool to find the prime factors of a positive integer is a factor tree. It doesn't matter whether we start by dividing 910 by 2 or by 5. The Fundamental Theorem of Arithmetic tells us that we'll get the same factors. Here's one way to factor 910:

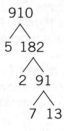

The prime factorization of 910 is $910 = 2 \times 5 \times 7 \times 13$. Based on the condition that $1 < r < s < t < u$, $r = 2$, $s = 5$, $t = 7$, and $u = 13$. Hence, the value of $u - s$ is $13 - 5 = 8$. The correct answer is (D).

Use Simple Numbers

Which of the following operations decreases the median of a list of distinct integers while leaving the standard deviation unchanged?

(A)   Multiplying each number in the list by 2

(B)   Multiplying each number in the list by $\dfrac{1}{2}$

(C)   Adding 0 to each number in the list

(D)   Adding $-\dfrac{1}{2}$ to each number in the list

(E)   Subtracting -2 from each number in the list

Solution: It sure would have been nice if the test-writers had provided the list of numbers, wouldn't it? Of course, we wouldn't want to actually calculate the standard deviation of the original list and the new lists created by the operations in each answer choice. After all, calculating standard deviations can be complicated and time-consuming. Moreover, neither the test-writers of the GMAT nor the GRE generally expect test-takers to calculate standard deviations. The test-writers are more interested in testing the concept, and that often means dealing with abstractions in problems.

Without the context of an actual list of numbers, the median and standard deviation[21] of a list of numbers certainly seems abstract. Of course, one way to deal with abstractions is to try to make the situation more concrete. We can do that by picking our own list of numbers. To do that, we need to first pay attention to any restrictions in the problem. We are told that the numbers are integers and that these integers are **distinct**, or different. However, notice that we weren't told whether the numbers are positive, negative, or a mix of both. We also weren't told whether the list includes zero.

When it comes to picking our numbers, we need to keep two things in mind. First, we'll start simple. There's no need to pick the craziest set of numbers that we can come up with. There may be only one answer left based on our simple set of numbers. Second, we'll be putting some faith in the question-writer. Questions on standardized tests such as the GMAT and GRE are very well vetted. The question-writer would have thought through all the possibilities. So, if there's only one answer left based on what happens with our simple set of numbers, we can go ahead and pick that answer.

Let's start with 1, 2, 3, 4, 5 as our list of numbers. These numbers have the advantage of being small and easy to work with. They also have an easy-to-calculate median, which is 3, and an easy-to-calculate average, which is also 3.

At this point, you may reasonably be saying "But the question didn't say anything about the average. Why did we just calculate the average?" Let's do a quick refresh on the concept of standard deviation. Standard deviation describes the dispersal of data about the mean.

---

[21]   For more information of medians, standard deviations, and other descriptive statistics, check out our bonus chapter in your online Student Tools.

When there are data points that are far from the mean, the standard deviation is large in comparison to the mean. When data points are all close to the mean, the standard deviation is small in comparison to the mean. Hence, even though we aren't going to calculate the standard deviation, it is helpful to know the mean of our list of integers so that we can get a sense of how the data is dispersed about the mean. For the numbers 1, 2, 3, 4, 5, we can see that all data points are no more than a distance of 2 from the mean.

Now, let's start evaluating the answer choices.

If we apply the operation from (A), the new list of numbers is 2, 4, 6, 8, 10. We can eliminate this answer choice because the median increased to 6, and we wanted the median to decrease. Moreover, we can also see that the data is more spread out. The new average is 6, and now there are data points that are a distance of 4 from the mean. Eliminate (A).

If we apply the operation from (B), the new list of numbers is $\frac{1}{2}$, 1, $\frac{3}{2}$, 2, $\frac{5}{2}$. Some of the new numbers are not integers, but that's not a reason to eliminate this answer choice. While the problem specified that the original list of numbers consists of integers, there is no requirement that the new list of numbers also be integers. For this new set of numbers, the median is $\frac{3}{2}$, so there has been a decrease. However, we can see that the new numbers are more tightly clustered around the new average, $\frac{3}{2}$, so the standard deviation has decreased. As we wanted the standard deviation to stay the same, we can eliminate (B).

At this point, we'll pause to note that multiplying every number in a data set by a constant other than 1 or −1 changes the standard deviation. Multiplying every number in a data set by numbers greater than 1 or less than −1 spreads the data out further. Multiplying by numbers between −1 and 0 or between 0 and 1 clusters the data more closely together. Multiplying every number in a dataset by zero makes the standard deviation of the new dataset zero. So, we could have eliminated (A) and (B) using this reasoning, too.

If we apply the operation from (C), the new list of numbers is 1, 2, 3, 4, 5. In this case, neither the median nor the standard deviation changed. Eliminate (C).

If we apply the operation from (D), the new list of numbers is $\frac{1}{2}, \frac{3}{2}, \frac{5}{2}, \frac{7}{2}, \frac{9}{2}$. The new median is $\frac{5}{2}$, so the median has decreased. The new average is $\frac{5}{2}$, and the data points show an equal degree of dispersal about this mean as the data points in the original list of numbers. Effectively, the data points have all just shifted the same amount to the left. So, the standard deviation is unchanged. Keep (D).

If we apply the operation from (E), the new list of numbers is 3, 4, 5, 6, 7. Note that subtracting −2 from each number is equivalent to adding 2 to each number. These numbers show the same degree of dispersal about their mean, 5, as the original list of numbers showed about their mean. So, the standard deviation has not changed. However, the median of this list of numbers, 5, is greater than the median of the original list of numbers, 3. So, the median has increased. Eliminate (E).

The correct answer is (D).

Remember All Possibilities

For a certain probability experiment, the probability that event H will occur is $\frac{1}{5}$ and the probability that event K will occur is $\frac{5}{8}$. Which of the following values could be the probability that the event $H \cap K$ (that is, the event H and K) both occur?

(A) $\frac{1}{6}$

(B) $\frac{1}{3}$

(C) $\frac{3}{8}$

(D) $\frac{1}{2}$

(E) $\frac{5}{8}$

Solution: Well, this problem is about as abstract as it can get, isn't it? Probability questions are usually about calculating the probability that some tangible event, such as getting at least two heads when flipping a coin four times, will happen. But this problem is about abstract events and there's a weird symbol!?! What's going on here?

Let's not panic. Even problems that deal with abstractions can seem more approachable on the second reading. We'll deal with the weird symbol first. The symbol is actually the symbol used in set theory to indicate the intersection of two sets. The intersection of two sets is a new set that contains only the elements that are in both sets. This symbol is also used in probability theory to indicate that two events both occur. However, the test-writers don't expect you to know that. So, they've included a brief definition of the symbol. As per the definition, the symbol is a stand-in for the word *and*. More simply, the last sentence of the problem could have been stated as *"Which of the following values could be the probability that the events H and K both occur?"*. Never put it past the test-writers to try to wring a little extra anxiety from the test-takers! That's why it's important to remember that any unusual symbols will be defined in the problem.

You may remember that the word *and* in a probability problem means to multiply the individual probabilities of events to get the probability of two or more events occurring. However, the product of the probabilities in the problem, $\frac{1}{5} \times \frac{5}{8} = \frac{1}{8}$, is not an answer choice. What's up with that? While it is true that $P(A \text{ and } B) = P(A) \times P(B)$, that rule is most often applied to the probability of a sequence of events. For example, we could use that rule to find that the probability of getting two heads when we flip a fair, two-sided coin two times is $P(HH) = \frac{1}{2} \times \frac{1}{2} = \frac{1}{4}$.

For this problem, however, we aren't necessarily looking at a sequence of events. So, we aren't just thinking about the probability that event *H* occurs followed by event *K* (or vice versa). Here, we also need to think about the probability of the two events occurring simultaneously. For example, we could envision event *H* being the probability of lightning during a storm and event *K* being the probability of rain. Rain and lightning can occur at the same time. However, rain can occur without lightning, and lightning can occur without rain.

The problem didn't state that we should consider only a sequence of events. So, we need to think about the more general case that H and K could occur at the same time. Great—now that that's settled, how do we think about the probability of the two events occurring simultaneously?

Probability theorists think of events as occupying an event space. The event space contains all the events that can happen for a given experiment. We don't need to get too into the weeds with this concept, but it can help us to conceptualize how to think about how our two events might interact. In fact, we need to think about three different cases. Thinking about how different cases affect a solution is also part of quantitative reasoning. In fact, we'll be closing this section with some additional problems that require us to think about different cases. So consider this problem a bit of foreshadowing!

Let's utilize circles to represent the probability that each of our events, H and K, occur. The circle represents the probability of each event on its own. Then we can think about the different ways that we can place these circles in our event space.

Case 1: No Overlap

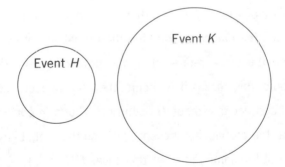

In this case, there's no overlap of the circles that represent the probability of each event. The interpretation of this case is that the two events are mutually exclusive. In other words, if H occurs, then K cannot occur. Also, if K occurs, then H cannot occur. We can include this possibility in our event space because the sum of the probabilities of the two events is less than 1: $P(H) + P(K) = \dfrac{1}{5} + \dfrac{5}{8} = \dfrac{33}{40}$. Because the events are mutually exclusive, the probability that they both occur simultaneously is 0. In symbols, $P(H \cap K) = 0$.

The test-writers could have given us 0 as an answer choice, but they didn't. We'll need to keep looking at different cases.

Case 2: Complete Overlap

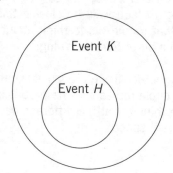

The probability of event H is less than the probability of event K. So, we could place the circle representing the probability of event H completely inside the circle representing the probability of event K. The interpretation of this case is if H occurs, then K also occurs. Note, however, that K can occur without H occurring. That's important because it means that the probability of event H is also the probability that both events occur at the same time. For this case, $P(H \cap K) = \dfrac{1}{5}$.

Again, the test-writers could have given us $\dfrac{1}{5}$ as an answer choice but didn't. So, we need to keep thinking about how we could arrange the two circles representing the probabilities of each event.

Case 3: Some overlap

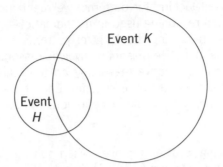

For this case, there is some overlap of the events. Event H can occur on its own. Event K can also occur on its own. Or, the two events can occur at the same time. It's important to understand that our diagram shows only one possibility for the degree of overlap of the two circles. We could move the circle for event H so that it is almost completely inside the circle for event K. Or, we could move the circle for event H so that only a very small amount of its area overlaps with that of event K.

So, for this case, there's a range of possible probabilities for the two events occurring at the same time. That range is limited by probabilities that we found in the previous two cases. We know what happens if we pull the circles completely apart. We also know what happens if we place the circle for event H inside the circle for event K. Therefore, the probability for this case is described by the inequality $0 < P(H \cap K) < \dfrac{1}{5}$.

We can also combine the probabilities for all three cases into the inequality $0 \le P(H \cap K) \le \dfrac{1}{5}$. So the correct answer could be any number in this range. The only answer in this range is $\dfrac{1}{6}$. The correct answer is (A).

Use Deductive Reasoning

When we discussed looking for patterns, we mentioned that there are two types of formal reasoning used in mathematics—inductive reasoning and deductive reasoning. Looking for patterns is part of inductive reasoning because inductive reasoning involves reasoning from the specific to the general. Deductive reasoning, on the other hand, involves reasoning from the general to the specific. Each time that you solve a math problem by applying a rule or definition, you are using deductive reasoning.

Deductive reasoning is also employed when solving problems that involve multiple steps. Moving from one step to the next often requires deductive reasoning. Some problems also provide some information, while the test-taker needs to provide some other information, such as rules or formulas that apply. These solutions require that deductions be made from the supplied information. Again, that's deductive reasoning in action!

Here are some problems that use deductive reasoning in their solutions.

Deductions with Rules and Formulas

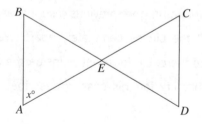

In the figure above, E is the midpoint of both segment AC and segment BD. If $AC = BD$ and $\angle CED = \frac{1}{2} \angle BEC$, then what is the value of x ?

(A) 30
(B) 45
(C) 50
(D) 60
(E) 75

Solution: Solutions to geometry problems often lean heavily on deductive reasoning. The problem supplies some information, and the test-taker uses geometry rules and formulas to deduce true statements, or conclusions, from that information. While the solutions to other types of problems also employ deductive reasoning, nowhere is that reasoning more integral than in geometry.

Let's go see what we can deduce!

If you watch people work on geometry questions, you might notice that people are more likely to sit and stare at them than an algebra or arithmetic problem. That's because it can be hard to know how to get a geometry problem started! A good first step is to redraw the provided figure,[22] then add any information that's in the problem but that isn't already shown on the figure.

In this problem, we are told that E is the midpoint of both segment AC and segment BD. We are also told that AC = BD. If we combine that information, it tells us that there are four segments that have equal length: AE = BE = CE = ED. We'll add the information from the problem to the figure by placing a tick mark on each of those segments. Here's what the marked-up figure looks like:

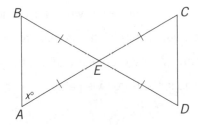

Now that we have some information, we can start thinking about what we know as a result. Sometimes it's helpful to ignore part of a geometry figure. In this case, let's ignore the right side of the figure, triangle CED. We're focusing on the left side of the figure because that's where the angle that we are interested in is. For a triangle, there's a rule that sides of equal length are opposite angles that have equal measure. Applying that rule to this triangle, we can deduce that ∠ABE and ∠BAE

---

[22]   Or draw a figure if one isn't provided and you think one will be useful!

have equal measure. We'll mark that on the figure by showing that both angles have measure $x°$.

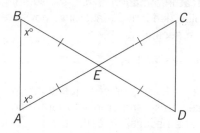

Now let's work with that other piece of information in the question stem: $\angle CED = \frac{1}{2}\angle BEC$. To work with this piece of information, we need to note that these angles are adjacent angles on line segment BD. That allows us to make use of another fact about lines and angles—the sum of the degree measures of adjacent angles on the same line is 180°. Due to this fact, we also know that $\angle BEC + \angle CED = 180$. If we think of the angles as variables, this latter equation contains two variables. We can't typically solve a single equation with two variables. However, we can make use of the relationship in the problem to rewrite this equation using only one variable. We can replace $\angle CED$ with $\frac{1}{2}\angle BEC$ based on the equation. After the substitution we get:

$$\angle BEC + \frac{1}{2}\angle BEC = 180$$

Remember that we are thinking about the angles as variables. These variables just have fancier names! But the equation above is equivalent to $y + \frac{1}{2}y = 180$. There's no rule that says that you have to call a variable x or y. To solve, we can just combine the coefficients to get:

$$\frac{3}{2}\angle BEC = 180$$

Then, multiply both sides of the equation by $\frac{2}{3}$ to find that $\angle BEC =$ 120°. Once we know the degree measure of $\angle BEC$, we can find that the degree measure of $\angle CED$ is 60°. It's a good practice to keep using the figure as you deduce new information. So, here's the updated figure:

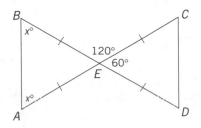

Now we can use another fact about lines and angles. When two lines intersect, the opposite (or vertical) angles have equal measure. Applied to this problem, this geometry fact lets us deduce that $\angle BEA = \angle CED =$ 60°. Again, we'll update the diagram.

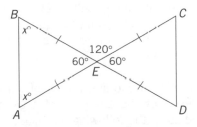

Finally, let's ignore the triangle on the right again. We'll be able to make use of the deduction that we made at the beginning of the solution that $\angle ABE = \angle BAE$, but first, we need one more geometry fact. The sum of the degree measures of the three angles in a triangle is 180°. In triangle ABE, we've already allocated 60°, and we know that the remaining 120° is split equally between the two remaining angles. Hence, $x = 60°$. We had to make use of a number of geometry rules and make a number of deductions but we found the value of x! The correct answer is (D).

Rethinking the Solution

Four people are playing a game in which each person rolls a six-sided die with faces numbered 1 to 6 at the same time. What is the probability that at least two of the people roll the same number?

(A) $\dfrac{1}{1296}$

(B) $\dfrac{1}{3}$

(C) $\dfrac{5}{18}$

(D) $\dfrac{2}{3}$

(E) $\dfrac{13}{18}$

Solution: This one is a bit daunting, isn't it? Even if you are comfortable with probability, you may be struggling to figure out how to do the calculation. How exactly do we account for the situations in which at least two of the people roll the same number?

Before we proceed, let's do a quick review of some probability concepts. Probability describes the chance that a given event will occur. Probability is defined using the following formula:

$$\text{Probability(event)} = \frac{\text{outcomes where event occurs}}{\text{all possible outcomes}}$$

For example, if you flip a coin that has two sides—one called heads for obvious reasons, and one called tails because what else are you going to match up with heads—the probability that the coin lands with heads facing up is $\dfrac{1}{2}$. The numerator of this fraction represents that there is only one outcome where the desired event occurs—the coin lands with heads facing up. The denominator represents that there are two possible outcomes—the coin lands with heads facing up or the coin lands with tails facing up.

The probability of an event ranges from 0 to 1. If the probability of an event is 0, it means that the event cannot happen. If the probability of an event is 1, it means that the event will definitely happen.

We need one more probability concept for this problem. Let's say that you are going to roll a six-sided die that has faces numbered 1 to 6. For whatever reason, you are interested in the probability that you roll a 4. The probability of rolling a 4 is $\frac{1}{6}$ because there is only one outcome of interest out of six possible outcomes. What's the probability that you roll something other than a 4? There are five outcomes of interest in this case because there are five numbers on the die that are not 4. There are still six possible outcomes so the probability of rolling a number other than a 4 is $\frac{5}{6}$. Now, notice that the sum of the probability of rolling a 4, $\frac{1}{6}$, and the probability of rolling something other than a 4, $\frac{5}{6}$, is 1. In other words, the probability of rolling a 4 is equal to the probability not rolling a 4 subtracted from 1. Here's what that looks like in equation form: $P(4) = 1 - P(\text{not } 4)$. We can generalize this rule, which is usually called the complement rule, as $P(A) = 1 - P(\text{not } A)$.

Okay, now that we've had a chance to review some probability concepts, let's start thinking about how to solve this problem. We could start by trying to list out all the ways that at least two people could roll the same number. For example, exactly two of the people could roll the same number. But which two? It looks like we'd need to account for multiple scenarios, such as the first and second person roll the same number but the third and fourth person roll a different number. We'd also need to account for cases where exactly 3 of the people roll the same number. And, when all four of the people roll the same number.

Now, however, we can pause to use a bit of deductive reasoning. If we care about exactly two of the people rolling the same number, and exactly three of the people rolling the same number, and all four of the people rolling the same number, it might be worthwhile to ask which situations we aren't interested in. Now that we've mapped out all the situations that we are interested in, we can deduce that there is only one situation that we are not interested in. Namely, the situation that all four people roll a different number.

Now we can use the complement rule: P(at least two roll the same number) = 1 − P(everybody rolls a different number). To find the probability that all four players roll a different number, let's imagine that they roll sequentially rather than all at once. This assumption won't change the outcome. It just makes it easier to think about the calculation.

The first person rolls the die, and this person can roll any of the six numbers. Nobody has rolled yet, so no numbers are excluded. So, the probability that the first person rolls a different number is $\frac{6}{6} = 1$.

Now, when the second person rolls, there are five numbers that are different from the number rolled by the first person. For example, if the first person had rolled a 4, then the second person can roll any of the numbers 1, 2, 3, 5, or 6, and have rolled a different number from the first person. So, the probability that the second person rolls a number that is different from that rolled by the first person is $\frac{5}{6}$.

When the third person rolls, there are four numbers that are different from those rolled by the first and second person. So, the probability that the third person rolls a different number is $\frac{4}{6}$.

When the fourth person rolls, there are three numbers that are different from those rolled by the first three people. So, the probability that the fourth person rolls a different number is $\frac{3}{6}$.

Now we need to introduce one more probability concept. We are trying to find the probability of a sequence of events. Here, the sequence of events can be thought of as each person rolling a number that is different from the numbers that were rolled by the people who rolled the die earlier. To find the sequence of an event, multiply the probabilities of each individual event in the sequence. Here's the finished calculation:

$$P(\text{at least 2 roll the same number}) =$$
$$1 - P(\text{everybody rolls a different number})$$

$$P(\text{at least 2 roll same number}) = 1 - \left(\frac{6}{6} \times \frac{5}{6} \times \frac{4}{6} \times \frac{3}{6} \right)$$

$$P(\text{at least 2 roll same number}) = 1 - \frac{5}{18} = \frac{13}{18}$$

The correct answer is (E).

Deductions from Definitions

For a certain distribution, the measurement 9.7 is $\frac{3}{4}$ standard deviations above the mean and the measurement 5.7 is $\frac{7}{4}$ standard deviations below the mean. What is the mean of the distribution?

(A) 8.4
(B) 8.5
(C) 8.6
(D) 8.7
(E) 8.8

Solutions: Here's another example where the problem supplies some information and we need to use facts and definitions about the standard deviation[23] concept to come to a conclusion from those facts. In this case, our conclusion is the mean of this distribution. Reasoning from the general to the specific is the essence of deductive reasoning.

---

[23] For more information on standard deviations and other descriptive statistics, check out our bonus chapter in your online Student Tools.

Because we'll be using the standard deviation concept in this problem, we'll take a minute to review a few key ideas. Standard deviation is a measure of distance from the mean of a set of data points. The standard deviation describes the spread of data about the mean. A large standard deviation means that the data is spread out far from the mean. A small standard deviation means that the data is tightly clustered about the mean. Most of the data in a distribution lies within one standard deviation of the mean.

This problem is hoping to confuse us by using fractional standard deviations and by stating that one measurement lies above the mean and one measurement lies below the mean. However, all we really need to use is the basic concept that standard deviation is a measure of distance. One standard deviation above the mean tells us what number we need to add to the mean to find a certain percentage of the data. If we know the data point at one standard deviation and we know the value of the standard deviation, we can find the mean. For example, let's say that we knew the standard deviation for a certain distribution is 2 and that the measurement 7 lies one standard deviation above the mean. In that case, we can find the mean by subtracting 2 from the measurement 7 to find that the mean is $7 - 2 = 5$.

So, one way forward is to determine the value of one standard deviation. To do that, we need to use the information provided in the problem along with what we know about the standard deviation concept. Let's see what deductions we can make. First off, we can determine the distance between the two measurements: $9.7 - 5.7 = 4$.

We can also determine how many standard deviations that distance between the two measurements represents. We do need to be careful here, because one measurement lies below the mean while the other lies above the mean. From the measurement that lies below the mean, we need to move $\frac{7}{4}$ standard deviations to get to the mean. For the measurement that lies above the mean, we need to move $\frac{3}{4}$ standard deviations from the mean to the measurement. Hence, to move from the measurement below the mean to the measurement above the mean, we need to move $\frac{7}{4} + \frac{3}{4} = \frac{10}{4} = \frac{5}{2}$ standard deviations.

That's a very helpful deduction that we've just made from the information provided by the problem. We now have a way to associate a certain distance, 4, with a certain standard deviation, $\frac{5}{2}$, for this distribution. Now we need to use that relationship to determine the distance that is equivalent to one standard deviation for this distribution. To do that, we can use the following proportion:

$$\frac{4}{\left(\frac{5}{2}\right) \text{ standard deviations}} = \frac{x}{1 \text{ standard deviation}}$$

Now, cross-multiply to find that $\frac{5}{2}x = 4$. So, $x = \frac{2}{5} \times 4 = \frac{8}{5}$. We have now determined that one standard deviation is equivalent to a distance of $\frac{8}{5}$.

Now we need to find the distance that corresponds to $\frac{3}{4}$ standard deviations. We could use either measurement for which we know the standard deviation, by the way. This choice was arbitrary. To find the distance that corresponds to $\frac{3}{4}$ standard deviation, we can set up another proportion.

$$\frac{\left(\frac{8}{5}\right)}{1 \text{ standard deviation}} = \frac{x}{\left(\frac{3}{4}\right) \text{ standard deviations}}$$

Now, cross-multiply to find that $x = \frac{8}{5} \times \frac{3}{4} = \frac{6}{5} = 1.2$. Now that we know the distance that $\frac{3}{4}$ standard deviation represents above the mean, we can find the mean by subtracting that distance from the measurement that we know lies $\frac{3}{4}$ standard deviations above the mean: $9.7 - 1.2 = 8.5$. The correct answer is (B).

By the way, you may have noticed that there's a way to solve this problem using only one proportion. We used two proportions to make the logic that we were using easier to see. But if you did see that you could use only one proportion, that's great! Remember that it's always good to think about different ways that you can solve problems!

Use Examples and Counterexamples

Humans like to make blanket generalizations. For math, many of us have a go-to number. It's often the number 2. If we want to test a rule, property, or operation, we try it with the number 2. Then, we assume that whatever is true for 2 is true for every other number. Of course, math doesn't work that way. There are many, many more numbers, and many rules, properties, and operations work differently for different types of numbers.

For example, what happens if you square a number? Did you say that it gets bigger? While it's certainly true that when you square 2 the result is a number that is greater than 2, it's not true that squaring a number always results in a greater number. If you square 1, you get 1, which is clearly not greater than 1. If you square $\frac{1}{2}$, the result is $\frac{1}{4}$, which is less than $\frac{1}{2}$. So, it's not true that we can be content to only test a rule or operation against the number 2.

Still, if you were to stand on a street corner and ask everyone who came by to give you a number, most people would give you numbers such as 2, 5, or 10. You'd ask a lot of people before someone said $\frac{1}{2}$ or −3 or π. Those are all valid responses. After all, you didn't ask for a positive integer. You asked for a number. Still, most of us equate the word "number" with a positive integer.

Mathematicians often need to think about exceptions and the different ways that rules work depending on the class of number under consideration, however. Part of proving a result often involves showing that there are no exceptions to that result. So you can probably see the interest that the test-writers have in this aspect of quantitative reasoning. Part of good quantitative reasoning involves being careful. It's necessary to consider all the possibilities. In other words, you need to realize that the universe of math extends beyond the number 2!

Here are some ways that the need to think about both examples and counterexamples shows up in problems.

Must Be

> If a and b are distinct positive integers, and a is even, then which of the following must also be even?
>
> (A) $2(a + b) - 3$
> (B) $(a - b) + 2$
> (C) $a + b - 1$
> (D) $a - b$
> (E) $ab - 2$

Solution: One way to approach this problem is to try different examples of values for the variables a and b. Of course, when we pick our examples, we need to make sure that the values we choose satisfy the conditions in the problem. For this problem, there are several conditions that must be observed simultaneously. We need to choose positive integers for both a and b. We need to choose different values for a and b. We need to choose an even integer for the value of a. Once we choose values for a and b, we can simply eliminate any answer choice that does not evaluate to an even integer with those values.

For example, let $a = 2$ and $b = 3$. Those numbers satisfy the conditions in the problem. With these numbers

Choice (A) is $2(2 + 3) - 3 = 7$, which is odd. Eliminate (A).

Choice (B) is $(2 - 3) + 2 = 1$, which is odd. Eliminate (B).

Choice (C) is $2 + 3 - 1 = 4$, which is even. Keep (C).

Choice (D) is $2 - 3 = -1$, which is odd. Eliminate (D).

Choice (E) is $(2)(3) - 2 = 4$, which is even. Keep (E).

At this point, we have found that three answers could be odd and that two answers could be even. However, we have only looked at one example of numbers that satisfies the conditions in the problem. We can eliminate the answers that could be odd because that single occurrence is sufficient to prove that the expressions in those answers do not produce a result that must be even.

For the two remaining answer choices, we need to evaluate them using different numbers. Effectively, we are trying to find a counterexample for which one of the remaining answers evaluates to an odd number. The best way to do that is to try the most different numbers that we can for a and b. The problem ties our hands for the value of a. We must choose an even number for a. As one even number is likely as good as any other even number, we'll leave the value of a alone. For b, however, we need a different type of number. Problems often contain clues about what different types of numbers we should consider. This problem limits us to using integers, one of the values can only be an even integer, and the correct answer must always evaluate to an even integer. We should clearly be thinking about even and odd integers. We've already tried an odd integer for b so let's try an even integer this time.

For this example, let's choose $a = 2$ and $b = 4$. We know from the previous example that (A), (B), and (D) don't *always* evaluate to even integers, so we only need to evaluate (C) and (E) for this example.

Choice (C) is $2 + 4 - 1 = 5$, an odd integer. Eliminate (C).

Choice (E) is $(2)(4) - 2 = 6$, an even integer.

Choice (E) is the only choice that evaluates to an even integer with both sets of numbers. The correct answer is (E).

Cannot Be

Which of the following CANNOT be the median of the five positive integers r, s, t, u, and v ?

(A) r

(B) u

(C) $r + t + v$

(D) $\dfrac{r + v}{2}$

(E) $\dfrac{r + s + v}{3}$

Solution: Here's a question that mixes a couple of the quantitative reasoning skills that we've been discussing. First off, this question requires the test-taker to work with abstract concepts. After all, problems about medians[24] typically deal with numbers, not variables and algebraic expressions.

Now, note the wording of the question. That capitalized word CANNOT looms large in the solution to this question. As a result, it's important to understand what that word means in terms of the solution and the strategy we'll employ to find the solution. The word *cannot* in this question indicates that four of the answer choices *can* be the solution while one answer choice can *never* be the median. It can be harder to look for something that is impossible, so our solution strategy here is to determine which answer choices can be the solution and eliminate those choices. To determine which answer choices can be the solution, we'll find an example of values for the variables that make that answer choice the median. We'll only need one example to prove that the answer choice can be the median. If we can successfully find examples for four of the answers, that means that we can pick the remaining answer choice without determining the reason that it cannot be the

---

[24] For more on medians and other descriptive statistics, check out your online Student Tools.

median. The person who wrote the question had to determine the reasons that the remaining answer couldn't be the median, but that was the writer's job rather than our job.

For (A), we can set $s = 1$, $t = 2$, $r = 3$, $u = 4$, and $v = 5$. Clearly, r can be the median, so we can eliminate (A). Note, by the way, that the variables being listed in alphabetical order in the problem does not imply that the values held by the variables need to be in numerical order. So we are free to assign numbers to the variables in whichever order accomplishes our purpose. Of course, we do need to assign only positive integers to the variables in order to satisfy the restriction in the question stem.

For (B), we can set $r = 1$, $s = 2$, $u = 3$, $t = 4$, and $v = 5$. This example shows that u can be the median, so eliminate (B).

Hm, (C). This one seems problematic. Consecutive integers such as 1, 2, 3, 4, and 5 don't seem to work no matter the order in which those numbers are assigned to the variables. It also doesn't seem to be the case that we can cluster three of the integers close together and make the other two integers greater to produce a list of numbers such as 1, 2, 3, 10, 15. Let's leave (C). This could turn out to be the answer if we can find examples to eliminate (D) and (E).

For (D), we can set $r = 1$, $s = 2$, $t = 3$, $u = 4$, and $v = 5$. The median of this list of numbers is 3. Choice (D) evaluates to $\dfrac{1+5}{2} = 3$, so we have found an example that shows that this choice can be the median. Eliminate (D).

For (E), we can set $r = 1$, $s = 2$, $t = 4$, $u = 5$, and $v = 9$. The median of this list of numbers is 4. Choice (E) evaluates to $\dfrac{1+2+9}{3} = 4$, so we have found an example that shows that this choice can be the median. Eliminate (E).

The correct answer is (C).

We have found the answer by process of elimination, and that's a perfectly valid way to find the answer. That's particularly true when the clock is ticking!

As for (C), we aren't required to find a reason that it cannot be the median. After all, there's no box on the test where we enter our reason. However, here's the reason. Consider any list of 5 different positive integers. For example, 1, 2, 3, 4, and 5. For this list, the median is 3. The sum of any 3 of these integers must be greater than the value of the third number in the list. What if some or all the integers were the same? Consider the list 1, 1, 2, 3, and 4. Again, the median is 2, but the sum of any three of these numbers is greater than the third number in the list. The same is true if we make all the numbers the same. For example, if the list is 1, 1, 1, 1, and 1, the median is 1 and the sum of any three numbers in the list is greater than the median. The restriction in the question that we only use positive integers makes it impossible for the sum of three of those integers to equal the third number in the list.

Not that we had to come up with that reason to answer the question!

Could Be

If $x > 1$ and $0 < y < 1$, which of the following could be 1 ?

(A) $\left(\dfrac{x}{y}\right)^2$

(B) $x^2 y^3$

(C) $x^2 + y^2$

(D) $x^2 + x^2 y$

(E) $x^2 + \dfrac{x^2}{y^2}$

Solution: To find an efficient way to solve this question, we need to take a moment to discuss the logic of this question. Unlike the correct answer to a question that asks for something that *must* happen, for which the desired answer works for every number that satisfies any conditions in the problem, the correct answer to a question that asks for something that *could* happen may only produce the desired result for one number (or set of numbers) that satisfies any conditions in the problem. That means that we may have trouble finding the number or set of numbers that produces the desired result.

Moreover, it's harder to eliminate answer choices. For a question that asks about a condition that must be true, all we need is one counter-example to eliminate an answer. For example, if a question asks us to find the answer that is always even and we find an answer that evalu-ates to an odd number for an allowed set of numbers, then we can eliminate that answer. The word *could* is a lot weaker than the word *must*, however. If we were asked to find an answer that could be even and we find that an answer evaluates to an odd number for a set of allowed numbers, we can't eliminate the answer choice. After all, that answer may evaluate to an even number for a different set of allowed numbers.

In other words, solving questions that ask us to find an answer that must be true is about finding counterexamples for the wrong answers. However, solving a question that asks us to find an answer that could be true, or could be equal to a certain number, is about finding an example that makes the correct answer meet that condition. Because it may be time-consuming to find that example, questions that use the word *could* often force us to depend on some form of reasoning or analysis to find the answer. Starting with some numbers might help us to understand the situation better, but those numbers are unlikely to help us find the answer unless we get lucky.

So, we'll proceed by using a combination of algebraic analysis, algebraic manipulation, and some numerical examples. Algebraic analy-sis is different than algebraic manipulation. Algebraic manipulation is what most people think of when they hear the word algebra. Algebraic manipulation is the skill that we use when we solve an equation. It involves well-known rules such as "group like terms" and "whatever is done to one side of an equation must be done to the other side of the equation." Algebraic analysis, on the other hand, involves thinking about the types of numbers that might make a given situation possible. Let's see how that works for the answer choices for this problem.

For (A), let's start by getting a sense of how this expression behaves

by picking some numbers for x and y. We'll stick to easy numbers and make $x = 3$ and $y = \dfrac{1}{2}$. With these numbers, this expression evaluates

to $\left(\dfrac{3}{\left(\dfrac{1}{2}\right)}\right)^2 = (3 \times 2)^2 = 6^2 = 36$. Those numbers certainly didn't make

the expression equal 1, but the real question is whether this expression

equals 1 given the restrictions in the question stem. Let's employ some

algebraic analysis. From the question stem, we know that $x > 1$ and

that y is a **proper fraction**. Our example helps us to see that, for these

restrictions, when x, a number greater than 1, is divided by y, a proper

fraction, the result is a number that is greater than x. Hence, we can

conclude that this expression results in a number greater than 1 getting

squared. For $x > 1$, the rule for squaring numbers in this range is that

$x^2 > x$, so we can conclude that the expression in (A) cannot equal 1,

given the restrictions in the question stem. Eliminate (A).

For (B), we can again start with exploring what happens when we assign

some easy numbers to x and y. Again, we'll use $x = 3$ and $y = \dfrac{1}{2}$. The

expression evaluates to $(3)^2 \left(\dfrac{1}{2}\right)^3 = (9)\left(\dfrac{1}{8}\right) = \dfrac{9}{8}$. Our result is close

to 1, and that gives us some reason to believe that the result could

equal 1 for some numbers x and y. We could try to rewrite one variable in terms of the other. However, remember that test-writers are more interested in concepts than calculations. There may be a reason that they chose to square one variable and cube another. As it happens, 64 is both a **perfect square** and a **perfect cube,** and that fact provides the example we need. If we make $x = 8$ and $y = \dfrac{1}{4}$, here's what happens when we evaluate the expression: $(8)^2 \left(\dfrac{1}{4}\right)^3 = (64)\left(\dfrac{1}{64}\right) = 1$. So, (B) can equal 1, and that means that (B) is the correct answer.

On the test, we could stop at (B). We've found the answer. However, let's go take a look at the remaining answer choices so we can practice how we should look at those.

For (C), we can again start with the same numbers that we used for (A) and (B). The expression evaluates to $3^2 + \left(\dfrac{1}{2}\right)^2 = 9 + \dfrac{1}{4} = 9\dfrac{1}{4}$. Now that our example has given us some insight into how this expression behaves, we can apply some analysis to conclude that this choice cannot equal 1. For $x > 1$, the rule for squaring numbers in this range is that $x^2 > x$, so the first part of the expression is greater than 1. To that, we'll add a fraction. As a result, this expression cannot equal 1 with the constraints on the variables. Eliminate (C).

For (D), we can start with the same numbers for x and y. The expression evaluates to $3^2 + \left(3^2\right)\left(\dfrac{1}{2}\right) = 9 + \dfrac{9}{4}$. The first part of the expression again will always evaluate to a number that is greater than 1. To that, we'll add another number. Again, we can conclude that this answer cannot equal 1, given the constraints. Eliminate (D).

For (E), we'll start with the numbers again. Surprise! The expression

evaluates to $3^2 + \left(\dfrac{3^2}{\left(\dfrac{1}{2}\right)^2} \right) = 9 + \left(\dfrac{9}{\left(\dfrac{1}{4}\right)} \right) = 9 + 36 = 45$. The example

helps us to get an idea of how the expression behaves. The first part,

for reasons we've already seen, evaluates to a number greater than 1.

To that, we'll be adding another number. This expression cannot equal

1, given the constraints. Eliminate (E).

The correct answer is (B).

Consider Different Cases

Closely related to the skill of considering examples and counterexam
ples is the skill of considering different cases. There are many situations in mathematics that lead to different cases. For example, if there
are two variables in a problem, it may be necessary to consider what
happens if both variables are positive, or both are negative, or one is
positive while the other is negative. Potentially, the use of two different
variables in a question may lead to the consideration of four different
cases.

This sort of reasoning is commonplace in math. Hence, the test-writers
view the ability to consider different cases an important part of quantitative reasoning. Some problems make the need to consider different
cases explicit by using multiple variables or by using words such as
could or *must* in the question stem. In other problems, the need to
consider different cases may be harder to detect. However, it's always
good to keep asking yourself if there's anything else that you need to
consider when solving a math problem.

Below are three different cases of the need to consider different cases.

Using Rules of Operations

If the quotient $\dfrac{x}{y}$ is positive, which of the following CANNOT be true?

(A) $x > 0$
(B) $y > 0$
(C) $xy < 0$
(D) $x - y > 0$
(E) $x + y < 0$

Solution 1: Here's another problem that includes the word CANNOT. As with the earlier problem, that word means that four of the answer choices can be true and one answer, the correct answer, is not true. For our solution, however, we'll use a different strategy.

In various sections, we've discussed how we need to think about how different operations work when applied to different sets of numbers. In other words, there were different cases to consider. That's the approach we will take for this problem.

There are two ways for the quotient $\dfrac{x}{y}$ to be positive. The first case is for both x and y to be positive. The second case is for both x and y to be negative. If one variable is positive and the other variable negative, then the condition of the problem, that the quotient be positive, is not met. So we only need to consider two cases.

We'll consider each case separately and eliminate any answer choices that can be true for that case.

Case 1: x and y are both positive.

If both x and y are positive, we can see that both answer (A) and (B) can be true. Because these choices can be true, they can be eliminated.

Choice (C) is not true for this case as the product of two positive numbers is positive. We can't eliminate this choice based on this case.

If $x > y$, then (D) can be true for this case. Eliminate (D).

Choice (E) is not true for this case as the sum of two positive numbers is a positive number.

Case 2: x and y are both negative.

We only have two answers left, so we only need to consider those choices for this case.

Choice (C) is not true for this case as the product of two negative numbers is positive. Since this choice was not true for both cases, we have shown that (C) cannot be true based on the restriction in the problem. The correct answer is (C).

We don't really need to eliminate (E) because we have shown that (C) is not true for both cases. However, if we were unsure, checking (E) could serve as a way to make sure that our earlier reasoning was correct.

Choice (E) is true for this case because the sum of two negative numbers is negative. Eliminate (E).

Solution 2: If solution 1 seemed too abstract, here's another way to solve this problem. We can apply the same principles of checking cases but use examples of each case.

For example, we can start by making $x = 4$ and $y = 2$. With these numbers, we can eliminate answers (A), (B) and (D).

Now we need some additional numbers that satisfy the condition in the problem. This time, however, we want to think in terms of how we can choose numbers that have different characteristics while still satisfying the condition in the problem. That leads us to the idea that we can choose negative numbers for x and y. For example, we can make $x = -4$ and $y = -2$. Now we can eliminate (E).

The correct answer is (C).

Think Beyond Symmetry

The sum of 13 different integers is zero. What is the greatest number of these integers that can be negative?

(A)   5
(B)   6
(C)   7
(D)   12
(E)   13

Solution: We'll need to consider different ways that the 13 integers can have a sum of zero.

Our first impulse might be to think in terms of symmetry. To build our list of integers, we might think that each time we add a negative number to the list, we need to balance it out with the corresponding positive number. In other words, we'd add pairs of additive inverses to the list. That would give us six pairs of additive inverses for a total of 12 integers. Then, we could just add zero to the list as the thirteenth number. So, we should choose (B), 6, right?

Well, not so fast. Symmetry is a wonderful thing. Mathematicians love to find symmetry. However, like any tool, symmetry must be applied in the right circumstances. Note that this question asks for the greatest number of integers that can be negative. So, this symmetrical distribution of the integers may not be the case that we want. We need to consider other ways that we could list out the numbers.

What if we decided to add a positive number that was the additive inverse of the sum of two of the negative numbers? For example, let's say that we decided to include −1 and −2 in our list of numbers. Rather than adding both 1 and 2 to our list to have four numbers with a sum of zero, we could add 3 to our list and have only three numbers that have a sum of zero.

Of course, we can add one positive number that is the sum of two of the negative numbers, or we can add one positive number that is the sum of three of the negative numbers. Or, four of the negative numbers. Or, well, you get the idea.

The case that will produce the greatest number of negative integers is to choose twelve negative integers and one positive integer that is the additive inverse of the sum of those twelve negative integers. For example, our thirteen integers could consist of the negative integers from −12 to −1 and the positive integer 78. The twelve negative integers have a sum of −78, so these thirteen integers have a sum of −78 + 78 = 0. The correct answer is (D).

Using Cases to Find the Approach

An antiques collector has 22 pairs of matched salt and pepper shakers. If 17 individual shakers are lost or broken during a move, what is the greatest number of pairs of matched salt and pepper shakers that the collector can have left?

(A)   5
(B)   8
(C)   12
(D)   13
(E)   14

Solution: So, here's a classic quantitative reasoning problem. The actual math required to solve the problem doesn't extend beyond basic arithmetic. However, the problem still leaves many a test-taker mightily flummoxed.

Remember that Pigeonhole Principle that we discussed at the beginning of this book? That can help guide our solution process here. We'll also consider some different cases until we find the logic for the path that will leave the collector with the greatest number of matched pairs of salt and pepper shakers.

At the beginning of the problem, we can think of the situation as the salt and pepper shakers have been divided into 22 boxes or "pigeon holes." Each of the boxes contains one salt shaker and one pepper shaker, and the salt and pepper shaker in each box contains a matched pair.[25]

---

[25]   Some of the matched pairs are hideous, by the way!

We might start working on the solution by deciding to remove one salt or pepper shaker from the first 17 boxes. That would leave us with 5 matched pairs. That's an answer choice so we're done, right?

Well, not so fast. Doesn't that answer seem a little too easy? The problem didn't ask us to determine how many matched pairs *could* be left. We were asked to find the *greatest* number of matched pairs that could be left. So, while we know that this case (aka removing an individual shaker) works, we have a strong suspicion that there are other ways to remove the shakers, and one of those ways likely results in more matched pairs being left.

We need to note the wording of the problem carefully. The problem states that individual salt or pepper shakers are removed. Can we take both the salt and pepper shaker from a box? Yes, we can, and doing so will result in more matched pairs being left.

Let's try to remove both the salt and pepper shaker from as many of the boxes as possible. If we remove both the salt and pepper shaker from the first eight boxes, we've removed 16 individual salt or pepper shakers. We're supposed to remove 17 individual salt or pepper shakers, so we'll also need to remove either the salt or pepper shaker from the ninth box.

That means that boxes 10 through 22 still contain matched pairs of salt and pepper shakers. Now, be careful. You might be tempted to think $22 - 10 = 12$, but that operation will find the difference between the two numbers rather than count the number of boxes. Here's one way to look at this situation. If we simply subtract, we're not counting the first box. So, there are actually 13 boxes that still have matched pairs of salt and pepper shakers in them.

If you are still a bit confused by that last bit, think about it this way instead. We removed 8 pairs of salt and pepper shakers. That left us with 14 pairs. Then, we removed a salt or pepper shaker from one of those pairs. That left us with 13 matched pairs.

The correct answer is (D).

We'll end our section exploring how quantitative reasoning is tested in math questions on the GMAT and GRE with this question because, you know, symmetry.

Symmetry isn't just for math problems. It's for books, too!

PART IV

Glossary of Math Terms

Glossary of Math Terms

This section collects most of the math terms defined and used in this book. Most of these terms are used in math problems on both the GMAT and GRE. A few terms are not (or rarely) used on these tests but can still be important to know because they can be used to understand or define terms that are used in math problems on these tests.

You can use these definitions as a reference when reading this book. You can also use these definitions as a basis for making flashcards. However, keep in mind our discussion that you need to do more than memorize to do well on your test!

Absolute value: The distance that a number is from zero on the number line. Absolute value applies to any real number. Absolute values are always nonnegative because a distance cannot be negative. Some examples of absolute values include: $|2| = 2$, $|-2| = 2$, $\left|-\frac{1}{2}\right| = \frac{1}{2}$, $|0| = 0$, and $\left|-\sqrt{3}\right| = \sqrt{3}$.

Addition: The process of combining two or more numbers to find a sum. Addition is one of the six basic operations tested on the GMAT and GRE. Addition can be performed on real numbers and is the inverse operation of subtraction. Important rules for addition include:

- The sum of two positive real numbers is a positive real number.
  - *Special case:* The sum of two positive integers is a positive integer.
- The sum of two negative real numbers is a negative real number.
  - *Special case:* The sum of two negative integers is a negative integer.
- The sum of a positive real number and a negative real number can be either a positive real number, a negative real number, or zero, which is a real number, and also an integer that is neither positive nor negative.

- For each positive real number, *a*, there exists a negative real number, *b*, for which the sum of *a* and *b* is zero ($a + b = 0$).
  - *Special case:* For each positive integer, *a*, there exists a negative integer, *b*, for which the sum of *a* and *b* is zero ($a + b = 0$).
- The sum of any real number and zero is that real number. So, $a + 0 = a$, where *a* is any real number.
- The order in which two real numbers are added does not change the sum. So, $a + b = b + a$. This is referred to as the commutative property.
- The order in which three or more real numbers are added does not change the sum. So, $(a + b) + c = a + (b + c)$. This is referred to as the associative property.

Additive inverse: A real number that can be added to another real number to produce a sum of zero. Examples of additive inverses include -3 and 3, $\frac{1}{2}$ and $-\frac{1}{2}$, and $\sqrt{3}$ and $-\sqrt{3}$. While neither the GMAT nor the GRE is likely to use the term additive inverse, the concept gets tested in a variety of ways.

Anticommutative Property: A property of subtraction and division. For these operations, the order of the numbers matters to the result. For subtraction, $a - b \neq b - a$ unless $a = b$. For example, $5 - 2 \neq 2 - 5$. Furthermore, for subtraction, $a - b = -(b - a)$. Equivalently, $|a - b| = |b - a|$. For example, $5 - 2 = 3$ and $-(2 - 5) = -(-3) = 3$. Also, $|5 - 2| = |2 - 5| = 3$. For division, $a \div b \neq b \div a$, unless $a = b$. For example, $6 \div 2 \neq 2 \div 6$.

Associative Property: A property of addition and multiplication. For these operations, the order of three or more numbers does not matter to the result. For addition, $(a + b) + c = a + (b + c)$. For example $(2 + 3) + 4 = 2 + (3 + 4)$. For multiplication $(a \times b) \times c = a \times (b \times c)$. For example, $(2 \times 3) \times 4 = 2 \times (3 \times 4)$.

Base: The number to which an exponent is applied. For example, for 2^3, the base is 2. Any real number can serve as the base, including zero, fractions, negatives, and irrational numbers such as π.

Commutative Property: A property of addition and multiplication. For these operations, the order of the numbers doesn't matter to the result. For addition, $a + b = b + a$. For example, $2 + 3 = 3 + 2$. For multiplication, $a \times b = b \times a$. For example, $2 \times 3 = 3 \times 2$.

Cube Root: An operation performed on real numbers, the result of which is a number that, when multiplied by itself, three times produces the number under the radical. For example, $\sqrt[3]{8} = 2$, because $2 \times 2 \times 2 = 8$.

Cubing a number: The common term for raising a number to the third power. For example, "two cubed" means $2^3 = 8$.

Denominator: The bottom number in a fraction. This number represents the total number of parts available, or the whole. For example, in the fraction $\frac{2}{3}$, 3 is the denominator and represents that there are 3 parts in the whole.

Difference: The result of subtraction. In the subtraction problem $5 - 3 = 2$, 2 is the difference.

Distinct: A word used in math problems to indicate that two items are different. For example, 2 and 5 are distinct positive integers. They are also distinct prime numbers. The term is also sometimes applied to variables. For example, to say "a and b are distinct positive integers" is another way of saying "a and b are positive integers for which $a \neq b$."

Distributive Property: A property of multiplication over addition and subtraction which states that $a \times (b + c) = (a \times b) + (a \times c)$ and $a \times (b - c) = (a \times b) - (a \times c)$. For example, $2 \times (3 + 4) = (2 \times 3) + (2 \times 4)$ and $2 \times (3 - 4) = (2 \times 3) - (2 \times 4)$.

Divisible: An integer is said to be divisible by another integer if the result of division is an integer. For example, 6 is divisible by 2 because $6 \div 2 = 3$, but 5 is not divisible by 2 because $5 \div 2 = 2.5$.

Element: A member of a list or set. For example, in the list of numbers 2, 3, 3, 4, the elements are 2, 3, 3, and 4. The term *list* refers to the four numbers as a group while the term *elements* refers to the individual numbers.

Exponent: The small superscript number that follows the base. For example, for 2^3, the exponent is 3. When the exponent is an integer, it indicates the number of times to multiply the base by itself. For example, for 2^3, the exponent 3 indicates to multiply 2 by itself 3 times, so $2^3 = 2 \times 2 \times 2 = 8$. Exponents can also be negative numbers, fractions, or zero. In these cases, the exponent does not indicate repeated multiplication. Each of these cases is defined as follows:

- Negative exponents represent reciprocals: $x^{-n} = \dfrac{1}{x^n}$. For example, $3^{-2} = \dfrac{1}{3^2} = \dfrac{1}{9}$.

- Fractional exponents represent roots: $x^{\frac{a}{b}} = \sqrt[b]{x^a}$. For example, $2^{\frac{2}{3}} = \sqrt[3]{2^2}$.

- For all $x \neq 0$, $x^0 = 1$. Note that 0^0 is undefined.

There are 3 basic rules for working with exponents. You can remember these as the MADSPM Rules. These rules are:

- **M**ultiply – **A**dd: When multiplying quantities with the same base, add the exponents: $\left(x^a\right)\left(x^b\right) = x^{a+b}$. For example, $\left(x^2\right)\left(x^3\right) = x^{2+3} = x^5$.

- **D**ivide – **S**ubtract: When dividing quantities with the same base, subtract the exponents: $\dfrac{x^a}{x^b} = x^{a-b}$. For example, $\dfrac{x^5}{x^2} = x^{5-2} = x^3$.

- **P**ower – **M**ultiply: When a number with an exponent is raised to another exponent, multiply the exponents: $\left(x^a\right)^b = x^{ab}$. For example, $\left(x^2\right)^3 = x^{2\times3} = x^6$. Note that a corollary of this rule is that $\left(x^a\right)^b = \left(x^b\right)^a$. For example, $\left(x^2\right)^3 = \left(x^3\right)^2$.

There are some other rules about exponents that are helpful to know:

- When a positive integer exponent is applied to a fraction between 0 and 1, the result is a number that is less than the fraction to which the exponent was applied. For example, $\left(\frac{1}{2}\right)^2 = \frac{1}{2} \times \frac{1}{2} = \frac{1}{4}$ and $\frac{1}{4} < \frac{1}{2}$.

- A negative number raised to an even exponent yields a positive result. A negative number raised to an odd exponent yields a negative result. For example, $(-2)^2 = 4$ and $(-2)^3 = -8$.

- For all x, $1^x = 1$.

- Exponents distribute across multiplication. So, $(ab)^c = \left(a^c\right)\left(b^c\right)$. However, exponents do not distribute across addition or subtraction. So, $(a+b)^c \neq a^c + b^c$.

Fraction: A number written in the form $\frac{a}{b}$, where b is not zero. All integers can be written as fractions by simply putting the integer over 1. For example, 2 can be written as the fraction $\frac{2}{1}$. However, this expression is not unique. For example, 2 can also be written as the fraction $\frac{4}{2}$. Of course, fractions also include numbers that are usually thought of as fractions, such as $-\frac{1}{3}$, $\frac{1}{2}$, and $\frac{5}{2}$. Fractions can also be thought of as unfinished division problems. For example, the fraction $\frac{2}{3}$ expresses 2 divided by 3.

Fundamental Theorem of Arithmetic: (Also known as the Unique Prime Factorization Theorem): Every integer greater than 1 can be expressed in exactly one way as a product of primes. For example, $24 = 2 \times 2 \times 2 \times 3$ and $35 = 5 \times 7$.

Hypotenuse: The side of a right triangle that is opposite the right angle. The hypotenuse is the longest side of the right triangle.

Identity element: A number that, when used in an operation, leaves some other number unchanged. For example, 0 is the identity element of addition because $a + 0 = a$ for any value of a. The identity element for multiplication is 1.

Improper Fraction: A fraction that has no sense of decorum! Seriously, an improper fraction is a fraction of the form $\frac{a}{b}$, where $\left|\frac{a}{b}\right| \geq 1$. For example, $\frac{5}{2}$ and $\frac{3}{3}$ are improper fractions.

Integer: The positive or negative whole numbers, plus zero. Integers are the natural numbers plus the negatives of the natural numbers that are greater than zero. The integers are ... –2, –1, 0, 1, 2 ...

Inverse operation: An operation that reverses the effect of another operation. For example, subtracting 3 reverses the effect of adding 3. Inverse operations usually used on the GMAT and GRE are:

- Addition and subtraction
- Multiplication and division
- Squaring a number and taking its square root

Irrational Number: A number that lacks sound judgement! Seriously, an irrational number is any real number that cannot be written as a fraction, where the numerator is an integer and the denominator is a nonzero integer. Examples of irrational numbers include $\sqrt{2}$, $\sqrt{3}$, $\sqrt{6}$, and π. The square root of any positive integer that is not a perfect square is an irrational number.

Isosceles Right Triangle: Any right triangle in which the legs have equal length. An isosceles right triangle is also referred to as a 45-45-90 triangle.

Isosceles Triangle: Any triangle with at least two sides of equal length.

Legs of a Right Triangle: The two sides of a right triangle that form the right angle. The length of each leg of a right triangle is less than the length of the hypotenuse.

List: A collection of numbers or other elements for which there are some repeated elements. For example, 1, 2, 2, 4, 6 is a list of numbers. *List* refers to the numbers as a group, while the individual numbers, or members of the list, are called *elements*.

Lower bound: For a set of numbers, either the least number in that set or the greatest number that no member of the set can equal. For example, if $x \geq 4$, then 4 is the lower bound and the least member of the solution set. If $x > 4$, then 4 is the lower bound and the greatest value that no member of the solution set can equal.

Mixed Number: Another way to write an improper fraction. A mixed number consists of an integer part and a fractional part. For example, $2\frac{5}{6}$ is a mixed number. In effect, a mixed number represents the addition of an integer and a fraction without the addition operator between the two numbers. So, $2\frac{5}{6} = 2 + \frac{5}{6}$. Mixed numbers can be positive or negative. To work with mixed numbers, it's usually easiest convert them into improper fractions. To do that, multiply the integer by the denominator of the fraction, add the numerator of the fraction to that product, and place the product over the denominator of the fraction. For example, $2\frac{5}{6} = \frac{(2)(6)+5}{6} = \frac{17}{6}$.

Multiplication: The operation used on two or more real numbers to find a product. Multiplication is one of the six basic operations tested on the GMAT and GRE. Multiplication is the inverse operation of division. Important rules for multiplication include:

- There are 3 basic rules that describe whether the product of two real numbers is a positive or a negative real number.
  - Positive × Positive = Positive
  - Positive × Negative = Negative
    (Also, Negative × Positive = Negative)
  - Negative × Negative = Positive

- Multiplication over addition or subtraction uses the distributive property.
  - $a \times (b + c) = (a \times b) + (a \times c)$
  - $a \times (b - c) = (a \times b) - (a \times c)$
- The product of any real number and zero is zero. So, $a \times 0 = 0$, where a is any real number.
- The product of any real number and one is that real number. So, $a \times 1 = a$, where a is any real number.
- Multiplying a real number by -1 yields the additive inverse of that number. So, $a \times (-1) = -a$, where a is a real number.
- The order in which two real numbers are multiplied does not change the product. So, $a \times b = b \times a$. This is referred to as the commutative property.
- The order in which three or more real numbers are multiplied does not change the product. So, $(a \times b) \times c = a \times (b \times c)$. This is referred to as the associative property.

- For all real numbers x, such that $x \neq 0$, there exists a real number $\frac{1}{x}$, such that $x \left(\frac{1}{x} \right) = 1$. The number $\frac{1}{x}$ is called the multiplicative inverse or the reciprocal.
- Multiplication of two positive real numbers by a positive real number preserves the order of the two original numbers for the products. Multiplication of two positive real numbers by a negative real number reverses the order of the two original numbers for the products.
  - If a, b, and c are positive real numbers and $b > c$, then $ab > ac$.
  - If a is a negative real number and b and c are positive real numbers such that $b > c$, then $ab < ac$.

Multiplicative Inverse: The number that you can multiply any given non-zero real number by to get 1 as the product. Stated another way, for all real $x \neq 0$, the multiplicative inverse is the number $\frac{1}{x}$, such that $x \left(\frac{1}{x} \right) = 1$. For example, $\frac{1}{2}$ is the multiplicative inverse of 2 because $(2)\frac{1}{2} = 1$. The multiplicative inverse can also be called the reciprocal.

Natural Number: The counting numbers plus the number zero. The natural numbers are 0, 1, 2, 3, 4 ...

Nonnegative: Any real number that is either positive or zero. When test-writers use the term nonnegative, they are stating that zero must be considered when evaluating an expression.

Nonzero Integer: Any integer except zero.

Nonzero real number: Any real number except zero.

Numerator: The top number in a fraction. This number represents the number of parts out of the whole. For example, in the fraction $\frac{2}{3}$, 2 is the numerator and represents that there are 2 parts out of the whole, or total number of parts.

One: A number with special properties. One is often the counterexample necessary to show that a proposed rule does not apply in all cases. Rules that apply to one include:

- One is the first positive integer.
- One is **not** prime.
- One is the identity element for multiplication. (For all n, where n is a real number, $n \times 1 = n$.)
- One is the identity element for division. (For all n, where n is a real number, $n \div 1 = n$.) Note that the order matters here: unless $n = 1$, $n \div 1 \neq 1 \div n$.
- One is the first perfect square.
- One is also the first perfect cube.

- When used as the base for any real exponent, the result is 1. (For all x, $1^x = 1$). For example, $1^2 = 1^{-4} = 1^{\frac{1}{3}} = 1^{-\frac{1}{2}} = 1^0 = 1$
- $\sqrt{1} = 1$

Order of Operations: Established conventions for which operations take precedence over others—commonly known as PEMDAS. The following is the order of precedence:

- Parentheses
- Exponents
- Multiplication and Division (in order from left to right)
- Addition and Subtraction (in order from left to right)

Perfect Cube: An integer that is the result of multiplying an integer by itself three times. Perfect cubes can be positive, negative, or zero. For example, 8 is a perfect cube because $8 = 2 \times 2 \times 2$ and -8 is also a perfect cube because $-8 = -2 \times -2 \times -2$. However, the term *perfect cube* is often used to refer to positive perfect cubes. Perfect cubes that are positive integers have cube roots that are positive integers, while perfect cubes that are negative integers have cube roots that are negative integers. For example, $\sqrt[3]{8} = 2$ and $\sqrt[3]{-8} = -2$. For both the GMAT and GRE, it's good be able to recognize the nonnegative perfect cubes up to 6^3. Those perfect cubes are 0, 1, 8, 27, 64, 125, and 216.

Perfect Square: An integer that is the result of multiplying an integer by itself. Perfect squares have square roots that are nonnegative integers. For both the GMAT and GRE, it's good to be able to recognize the perfect squares up to 16^2. Those perfect squares are 0, 1, 4, 9, 16, 25, 36, 49, 64, 81, 100, 121, 144, 169, 196, 225, and 256.

Positive Number: Any real number greater than zero.

Prime Factor: A factor of a positive integer that is also prime.

Prime Factorization: The expression of a positive integer as a product of prime numbers.

Prime Number: A number that works for Amazon! Seriously, it's a positive integer greater than 1 that is divisible only by 1 and itself. For example, 7 is a prime number because its only divisors are 1 and 7. Important properties of prime numbers include:

- 1 is not prime.
- 2 is the only even prime.
- Prime numbers are not evenly distributed among the integers. For example, the difference between 5 and 3 is 2, but the difference between 11 and 7 is 4.
- Odd prime numbers greater than 5 have 1, 3, 7, or 9 as their units digits.

Product: The result of multiplication. In the multiplication problem $2 \times 5 = 10$, the product is 10.

Proper Fraction: A fraction that always behaves in an appropriate manner! Seriously, a proper fraction is a fraction in the form $\dfrac{a}{b}$ for which $\left|\dfrac{a}{b}\right| < 1$. In other words, a proper fraction is a fraction that is between 0 and 1. For example, $\dfrac{1}{2}$ is a proper fraction.

Pythagorean Theorem: The theorem that describes the relationship of the lengths of the three sides of a right triangle. In any right triangle, the lengths of the sides satisfy the formula $a^2 + b^2 = c^2$, where a and b are the lengths of the legs of the right triangle and c is the length of the hypotenuse of the right triangle. Did you notice that we kept saying right triangle in this definition? That's because the Pythagorean Theorem only applies to right triangles!

Quotient: The result of division. For example, in the division problem $6 \div 3 = 2$, the quotient is 2.

Range: A type of statistic used to indicate the dispersal of data in a set of observations. The range is the difference between the greatest and least values in a set of data. For example, if a dataset consists of the values $-10, -4, 0, 2, 5, 20$, the range is $20 - (-10) = 30$. However, the range doesn't provide any information about the distribution of numbers between the greatest and least values in a dataset.

Rational Number: Any real number that can be written as a fraction where the numerator is an integer and the denominator is a nonzero integer. All integers, including zero, are rational numbers, as are all fractions, including both proper and improper fractions. Examples of rational numbers include -3, 0, $\dfrac{1}{2}$, 2, and $\dfrac{5}{2}$.

Real Number: The set of numbers that includes both the rational numbers and the irrational numbers.

Reciprocal: The number that you can multiply any given nonzero real number by to get 1 as the product. Stated another way, for all real $x \neq 0$, the reciprocal is the number $\dfrac{1}{x}$, such that $x\left(\dfrac{1}{x}\right) = 1$. For example, $-\dfrac{1}{2}$ is the reciprocal of -2 because $(-2)\left(-\dfrac{1}{2}\right) = 1$. The reciprocal can also be called the multiplicative inverse.

Relational Operator: An operator that determines a relationship between two real numbers. The relational operators used on the GMAT and GRE are greater than ($>$), greater than or equal to ($\geq$), less than ($<$), less than or equal to ($\leq$), and equal to ($=$).

Relatively Prime: A term used to describe two positive integers that have no shared prime factors. For example, 4 and 15 are relatively prime because the prime factorization of 4 is $4 = 2^2$ and the prime factorization of 15 is $15 = 3 \times 5$. When two numbers are relatively prime, their least common multiple is their product. For example, the least common multiple of 4 and 15 is $4 \times 15 = 60$. Note that the term *relatively prime* does not imply that the integers themselves are prime. For example, neither 4 nor 15 is prime. However, two prime numbers are always relatively prime. For example, 3 and 7 are relatively prime, as well as being prime numbers.

Right Triangle: A triangle in which one of the angles has a degree measure of 90°. The sum of the degree measures of the other two angles is 90°. Two right triangles that frequently come up on both the GMAT and the GRE are the 30-60-90 and 45-45-90 right triangles. Note, however, that other right triangles such as a 20-70-90 are possible. The lengths of the sides on any right triangle satisfy the Pythagorean Theorem.

Set: A collection of items with each item being different from every other item. The notation for sets includes the elements, or members, of the set in braces: { }. So {1, 2, 3} is a set consisting of the three elements: 1, 2, and 3.

Square Root: An operation performed on nonnegative real numbers, the result of which is a number that, when multiplied by itself, produces the number under the radical. For example, $\sqrt{4} = 2$, because $2 \times 2 = 4$. For the purposes of the GMAT and GRE, the use of the square root symbol indicates that the result of the operation is nonnegative. When the GMAT or GRE wants both the positive and negative roots considered, they will generally provide an equation such as $x^2 = 4$, the solution to which is both 2 and –2. Occasionally, the ± symbol will appear before the radical.

Squaring a number: The common term for raising a number to the second power. For example, "two squared" means $2^2 = 4$.

Subtraction: The process of combining two or more numbers to find a difference. Subtraction is one of the six basic operations tested on the GMAT and GRE. Subtraction can be performed on real numbers and is the inverse operation of addition. Important rules for subtraction include:

- The difference of two real numbers can be a positive real number, a negative real number, or zero, which is a real number that is neither positive nor negative.
- The difference of any real number and zero is that real number. So, $a - 0 = a$, where a is any real number. However, $0 - a = -a$.

- Subtraction is not commutative. So, $a - b \neq b - a$ unless $a = b$. Subtraction is anticommutative.
- Subtraction is not associative. So, $(a - b) - c \neq a - (b - c)$.

Sum: The result of addition. In the addition problem $2 + 5 = 7$, the sum is 7.

Transitivity: A property of the five relational operators used on the GMAT and GRE. If a R b and b R c, then a R c, where R refers to one of the relational operators $>$, $\geq$, $<$, $\leq$. and $=$. For example, if $a > b$ and $b > c$, then $a > c$.

Unit Fraction: A fraction that has a numerator of 1. For example, $\frac{1}{2}$ and $\frac{1}{4}$ are unit fractions. Unit fractions are the reciprocals of positive integers.

Units Digit: The first digit to the left of the decimal point. Another name for the ones digit. For example, in the number 123.46, the units digit is 3. In the number 245, the units digit is 5.

Upper bound: For a set of numbers, either the greatest number in that set or the least number that no member of the set can equal. For example, if $x \leq 4$, then 4 is the upper bound and the greatest member of the solution set. If $x < 4$, then 4 is the upper bound and the least value that no member of the solution set can equal.

Well-ordered: A term describing a set in which each element has a successor, i.e., a next element.

Whole number: A number that has no fractional or decimal part. Whole numbers differ from natural numbers in that whole numbers can also be negative. For example, -2 is a whole number but not a natural number, whereas 2 is both a whole number and a natural number. Zero is also both a whole number and a natural number.

Zero: A number with special properties. Zero is often the counter-example necessary to show that a proposed rule does not apply in all cases. Rules that apply to zero include:

- Zero is an integer. (Because zero is an integer, it is also a rational number and a real number.)
- Zero is the only real number that is neither positive nor negative.
- Zero is an even integer.
- Zero is the identity element for addition. (For all n, where n is a real number, $n + 0 = n$.)
- Zero is the identity element for subtraction. (For all n, where n is a real number, $n - 0 = n$.) Note that the order matters here. Unless $n = 0$, $n - 0 \neq 0 - n$.
- The product of any real number and zero is zero. (For all n, where n is a real number, $n \times 0 = 0$.)
- Division by zero is undefined.
- $|0| = 0$ (The absolute value of 0 is 0.)
- When used as an exponent for any real number that is not zero, the result equals 1. (For all $x \neq 0$, $x^0 = 1$)
- $\sqrt{0} = 0$
- 0^0 is undefined.